The
Timewasting
Emails

AUTHOR'S ACKNOWLEDGEMENTS
To my mother and father – I hope this goes some way to saying sorry again for the fire incident.

Also to my main wind-up target – the long-suffering Lynn.

Finally, to all the teachers who repeatedly wrote on my report card, 'Raymond could do better' – I like to think I proved them wrong.

This edition published in 2015 by Prion
An imprint of The Carlton Publishing Group
20 Mortimer Street
London W1T 3JW

Previously published as *The Raymond Delauney Emails* in 2007

Text © 2007 Raymond Delauney
Design and layout © 2007 Carlton Publishing Group

ISBN 978-1-85375-926-0

Printed and bound by CPI Group (UK) Ltd, Croydon, CR0 4YY

The
Timewasting
Emails

Nuisance
Emails
from a Total
Pain in the Neck

Raymond Delauncy

PRION

CONTENTS

INTRODUCTION

I'd like to offer some rational, or psychological, explanation as to why I, Raymond Delauney of 4 Harold Wilson Close, Hammersmith W14, wilfully choose to annoy complete strangers. I put it down to that very good thing about today's society, namely: it is entirely possible to put the blame for absolutely anything on someone – anyone – other than yourself. But I've got to hold my hands up – and run round in circles. I think the plain, simple truth of the matter is that I get a sort of perverse pleasure by getting on people's nerves. I think wherever we are, we all secretly enjoy watching the harmless nutcase in the train carriage who harasses someone else. Luckily it's not just the same guy either, we're all over the place. After all, as my dear grandmother used to say, "If you can't laugh at others who can we laugh at?"

I've always been a fairly annoying person. When I was a youngster one of my earliest hobbies was to prove to people that I actually could count to a million, repeatedly.

I recall one occasion when I was only six years old. I was sitting on the porch when a salesman sauntered up the gravel drive and asked, "Hey son, is your mum home?" "She sure is," I replied. So he rang the doorbell five or six times, without answer. He eventually turned to me and said, "Hey son, I thought you said your mum was home." "She Is," I replied, "but I don't live here."

Of course, the time comes when you have to stop being an annoying little kid and mature into an annoying adult. I mean, what are adults if not bigger children?

I may have inherited the 'annoying gene' from my father. I could tell from an early age that he was the sort of fellow who liked to invite reaction. The type of chap people would point at. When he went to what our American cousins call 'drive thru' restaurants he'd insist on specifying that his order was "TO GO!" And when he queued up for something he liked to leave large gaps between himself and the people in front of him for no logical reason whatsoever. Whenever we ate out as a family he might casually enquire of the waiters if they were really bad singers or really bad actors. A possible downside of this was that I recall the food, when it eventually arrived, was generally very chewy or very runny.

Maybe it isn't my fault that I'm the way I am after all. So when some smart fellow came along and invented the Internet I saw it as a direct opportunity to reach out to people from all corners of the globe. And annoy them. I'm sure it's what the internet was truly invented for. After all, you can only look at so many dirty pictures.

Raymond Delauney,
London

CONTACT WITH A PSYCHIC

Delete | Reply ~ | Forward ~ | Spam | Move... ~

Date:	Wed, 7 Mar 2007 12:11:43 +0000 (GMT)
From:	"raymond delauney" <raymonddelauney@yahoo.co.uk>
Subject:	My Dilemma
To:	pennyhart@happymystic.com

Hi Penny,

I take my hat off to you for possessing special powers and availing them for the general betterment of the world.

Psychics like yourself are gifted people. I bet lots of people say 'a penny for your thoughts'. A funny joke I would venture, given the name and nature of your vocation. I am hoping you can help me with your thought power on an important issue that needs urgent resolution.

Let's get down to brass tacks:
I live in Scotland (though I am originally English). I have two twin brothers one, Roy, 40, who lives in Nova Scotia (Canada) and the other, Roger, also 40, who lives in Singapore (Asia).

Before my mother died she left me a valuable painting, which has somehow ended up in the possession of one of my brothers.

The watercolour is by the artist Henry Bernard Chalon and is estimated at around £25,000 in value. Mother wanted me to have the painting as I have an eye for intricate detail on expensive paintings. I believe I was her favourite (she always called me 'her Raymondo').

I distinctly recall mother saying the painting was at one of my brothers' houses, in his loft. But here's the problem: I can't remember which brother has it!

I don't want to ask either twin whether they have it over the phone in case they research the painting's value and become consumed with greed, which is a terrible thing. Both brothers are far better off than me, one is a chubby orthopaedist who owns three cars whilst the other works in the shipping industry has 2 ponies and a wife who spends more on her wardrobe than I do on my kids. So it's not as though they need the money.

My plan is to go and visit the bro who has the painting as part of a holiday. My wife could distract them by taking them out for a meal while I have a little rummage in the loft.

Once back with its rightful owner I aim to place the painting above my mantelpiece for a while so that I can feel closer to mum. After I get that contentment, and only after, will I put it up on eBay to ease my current financial plight.

I need to know which brother has the painting, as booking two holidays would be expensive – as well as time consuming. I haven't much money but if you could use your special powers to let me know which brother has my painting I will grease your palm with £250 of silver once I hawk it.

Will it be more difficult to tell who has it because they are twins and have similar genetic thought patterns?

Roy Delauney: date of birth 22/04/66. Height 6'. Hair colour brown. Wife's name: Lucy. Car: Volvo, MG, and a small car. Favourite sport: golf.

Roger Delauney: date of birth 22/04/66. Height 6'. Hair colour brown. Wife's name: Alison. Car: BMW. Favourite sport: tennis/golf.

Tip me the wink where the picture is and I'll look after you – but you already know that I guess, what with your special powers.

Many congratulations on your work so far, which has been excellent.

Thanks in advance,

Raymond Delauney

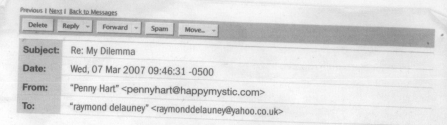

Subject:	Re: My Dilemma
Date:	Wed, 07 Mar 2007 09:46:31 -0500
From:	"Penny Hart" <pennyhart@happymystic.com>
To:	"raymond delauney" <raymonddelauney@yahoo.co.uk>

For a reading of this type I usually charge around $75.00, but also I do reduce my rates for people who cannot afford the higher price. I could look into this for you (I already have an idea which brother has it) using my guides and tell you of steps to take to assure that you get it from him also. For that I would only charge you $20.00.

That can be sent to me through PayPal.com using my email of pennyhart@happymystic.com. If you do not have PayPal I take all major credit cards and can send you an invoice through PayPal that will allow you to pay by credit card without signing up for a PayPal account. When payment is received I will send you the answer, just be sure to send me an email with your brother's name first and last in it also.

Hope to hear from you soon

Penny Hart

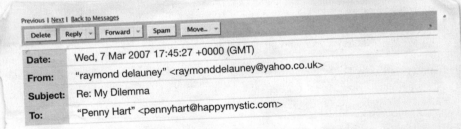

Date:	Wed, 7 Mar 2007 17:45:27 +0000 (GMT)
From:	"raymond delauney" <raymonddelauney@yahoo.co.uk>
Subject:	Re: My Dilemma
To:	"Penny Hart" <pennyhart@happymystic.com>

Penny,

Terrific news!!!

Did you like my joke about a 'penny for your thoughts'? I made it up myself.

It's interesting that you already have a sense of which brother might have the painting. I don't have a clue.

I'm pretty short of liquid funds at present so how does a 10 percent bonus sound?

That is to say if you give me the correct answer (and I promise I'll pay up) I'll give you 10 percent of whatever the painting is sold for.

I'll even let you watch the sale on eBay. But I guess you will have a rough idea of the value with your predictive powers!!

It should go for around £25,000 and so a 10 percent slice of that adds up to a juicy £250 or $500. That way everyone is happy.

Obviously it's a 50/50 chance for someone without your thought patterns. But with your skills I'd get the right answer straight away and you'd make some money.

We got ourselves a deal?

Raymond

Delete | Reply ▾ | Forward ▾ | Spam | Move... ▾

From:	"Penny Hart" <pennyhart@happymystic.com>
To:	"raymond delauney" <raymonddelauney@yahoo.co.uk>
Date:	Wed, 07 Mar 2007 14:16:02 -0500
Subject:	Re: My Dilemma

Sure fair enough deal :) when you put it on eBay be sure to send me the link so I can check it out :)

The one who has it is Roy. He has forgotten that he has it and if you aok him about it later you will find it stacked on its side in the attic with a box that has a red cloth or something red on it and tell him it would mean a lot to you and that you want it because it is mom's he will give it to you.

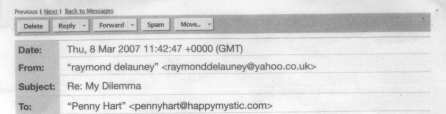

Date:	Thu, 8 Mar 2007 11:42:47 +0000 (GMT)
From:	"raymond delauney" <raymonddelauney@yahoo.co.uk>
Subject:	Re: My Dilemma
To:	"Penny Hart" <pennyhart@happymystic.com>

Terrific news!!!

I thought Roy may have had the painting but to have it confirmed by someone of your powers is damned well reassuring. I've just booked a flight to Canada.

Unfortunately the wife, or 'Saggy' as I call her, has insisted she comes along. She wouldn't want me enjoying myself. We tend to row a lot these days – she blames me for her having low esteem. Not sure where she gets that from.

The only point I would disagree with you on is that I very much doubt Roy would let me have the painting if he suspects it's cash convertible. He's as tight as a coat of paint. As a boy he could open and eat a packet of crisps silently and secretly in his pocket just so he didn't have to share them with me.

I'll get Saggy to have a root around the attic when I take Roy and his family out for a meal. No point in Roy demanding a piece of the picture – he's loaded anyway.

I'll make sure I cut you in for a juicy 10%. Should add up to a handy $250.

I just realised that with you being American you probably didn't understand my rib tickling 'penny for your thoughts' remark. You Americans use cents instead of pennies.

Thanks for your brilliant help,

Raymond

From:	"Penny Hart" <pennyhart@happymystic.com>
To:	"raymond delauney" <raymonddelauney@yahoo.co.uk>
Date:	Thu, 08 Mar 2007 08:53:52 -0500
Subject:	Re: My Dilemma

LOL I actually do understand your ribbing hun. I am known internationally so I talk to a wide range of people. For example in the US the word spoof means to copy or imitate something. I couldn't tell you what it means in "the land down under". It's too dirty LOL.

Ozzies have a great sense of humor.

| Delete | Reply ▼ | Forward ▼ | Spam | Move... ▼ |

Date:	Tue, 20 Mar 2007 12:10:07 +0000 (GMT)
From:	"raymond delauney" <raymonddelauney@yahoo.co.uk>
Subject:	Thanks a bunch
To:	"Penny Hart" <pennyhart@happymystic.com>

Remember me?

You probably don't.

Please allow me to remind you. I'm the plum you sent to Nova Scotia, Canada – in search of a valuable painting – a painting that wasn't there.

Do you get a kick sending people half way around the globe on a wild goose chase?

I made the HUGE mistake of believing you were a world-class medium.

Now, because of you, my brother doesn't want to see or hear from me ever again and the wife is sleeping on the couch.

Worse, much worse is the cost of the round trip hit me in the pocket to the tune of £3,000. I figure I should have that paid off by the back end of June – 2009.

My brother, Roy, ejected my wife and me from his house on day two of our planned ten-day stay. He doesn't want to see me again, ever.

I took Roy, his wife and their two kids for a slap up meal while my wife stayed behind on the pretext she was unwell with one of her headaches. The plan was for the missus to have a scout around the attic while the coast was clear.

Unfortunately, what wasn't in the plans was for my lard assed wife putting her foot through the plasterboard, making a huge foot shaped hole in the ceiling. It's something you can hardly blame on rats – which of course is exactly what she did.

The fact that her fat footprints, covered in plaster, led a tell tale trail all the way back to her room didn't help lend her story much in the way of credibility.

Of course, as she repeatedly reminds me, the whole thing would never have happened if you hadn't sent us on a wild goose chase in the first place.

My wife had to have 8 stitches inserted in her ankle, costing me £23 a stitch.

She eventually confessed it was her that caused the hole in the ceiling, emphasising the fact it was all my idea.

Roy went puce with rage, and then when he finally reddened down he got angry again and threw some punches at me. I had to put him in a headlock for my own protection whereupon he accidentally broke his collarbone.

Roy took great pleasure in telling me our other brother had the painting all along. He lives in Singapore, which isn't in the same continent as Nova Scotia, by the way.

What happened to us? Well, if you're interested Roy 'kindly' dropped us off at the hospital with our suitcases and the message never to contact him again.

The only good thing to come out of this is the wife is now kipping on the couch, she actually believes this is punishing me. I must say all the extra space I have to stretch out at night and not being able to hear her rasping snore is really teaching me a valuable lesson. When she 'can't be bothered to trim her nipple hair' you just know there's zero romance left in the marriage.

So, thanks to you, my marriage is in tatters, both my brothers hate me and my bank balance is £3,000 lighter.

Without your useless, duff, no good, pathetic advice I'd never have travelled to Canada in the first place.

How do you have the cheek to call yourself a medium, you look more like an extra large to me, anyway.

You have ruined my life.

Raymond Delauney

Delete | Reply ▾ | Forward ▾ | Spam | Move... ▾

From:	"Penny Hart" <pennyhart@happymystic.com>
To:	"raymond delauney" <raymonddelauney@yahoo.co.uk>
Date:	Tue, 20 Mar 2007 08:09:41 -0500
Subject:	Re: Thanks a bunch

First of all don't you ever, ever send this office an email like this again. Who the hell do you think you are?! You beg for my help and then treat me like dirt! Learn some respect. I went by what my guides told me and my guides are never ever wrong!

Maybe, just maybe, instead of trying to con or steal something from your brothers that you think is yours, but have no proof it was given to you, maybe you should have just asked them for it.

I would say since you were lying to them and trying to steal from them and also went through their home searching without their consent then you and your wife got exactly what you deserve!

I am a well-known world-renowned psychic. Am I perfect? No! But two things I don't do is steal and lie! You apparently can't say the same thing now can you!

Next time beg Sylvia Browne for help!

Date:	Wed, 21 Mar 2007 11:30:48 +0000 (GMT)
From:	"raymond delauney" <raymonddelauney@yahoo.co.uk>
Subject:	Re: Thanks a bunch
To:	"Penny Hart" <pennyhart@happymystic.com>

Penny

This really takes the biscuit.

I mean, it really does.

If my life wasn't such a car wreck I'd probably find this funny.

I really struck oil when I enlisted the services of a 'world-renowned' guide.

My guess is the only guide you've got hanging around the trailer belongs to your husband and is of the Labrador variety.

Frankly I think I'd have been better off talking to the other dumb mutt.

I doubt you could even successfully predict what day of the week it is.

What qualifications do you need to do your job anyway? Watch Ghostbusters a couple of times and get some references off a couple of stiffs?

And another thing, if you're as good as you claim to be how come you ain't coming up on the lotto every other week?

You have the cheek to call me a crook but you put your name down for a 10% slice of the proceeds. Luckily, I was never going to pay you that anyway.

If your guides are never wrong maybe I should have emailed them in the first place. Instead I get the middleman. Is that why you're called mediums?

I wish you all the luck – with your lack of foresight you sure are going to need it.

Regards,

Raymond Delauney

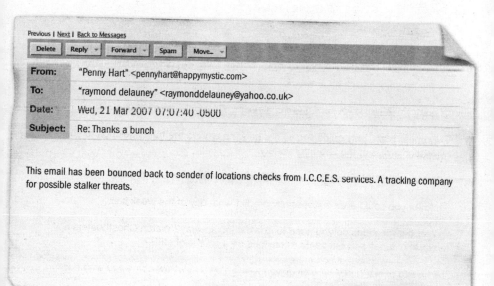

| Delete | Reply ▾ | Forward ▾ | Spam | Move... ▾ |

From:	"Penny Hart" <pennyhart@happymystic.com>
To:	"raymond delauney" <raymonddelauney@yahoo.co.uk>
Date:	Wed, 21 Mar 2007 07:07:40 -0500
Subject:	Re: Thanks a bunch

This email has been bounced back to sender of locations checks from I.C.C.E.S. services. A tracking company for possible stalker threats.

END OF CORRESPONDENCE

DOORMAN

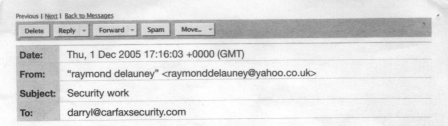

| Delete | Reply ▾ | Forward ▾ | Spam | Move... ▾ |

Date: Thu, 1 Dec 2005 17:16:03 +0000 (GMT)

From: "raymond delauney" <raymonddelauney@yahoo.co.uk>

Subject: Security work

To: darryl@carfaxsecurity.com

Hi,

I saw the advert for security staff. I think I fit the bill.

I don't have no security experience what you might want but I have worked on the front line at many clubs.

I've work the door at Wall to Wall in Bromley for two years and can provide good references if required.

Basically, if it goes off you can rely on me. If any other staff are in trouble I'll wade in. I don't look for it but will 'ave it if they want to get busy.

I'm 6'3 high. When I hit someone they stay hit. I doubt anyone else what applies will be able to bench press more than me.

We get a load of students where I work but they are mainly pussies, sometimes I might need to crack a few heads together though.

I don't like trouble but I don't turn and walk away from it.

How much is the pay?

Raymond Delauney

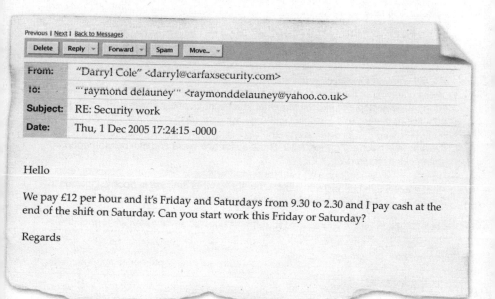

Delete | Reply ▾ | Forward ▾ | Spam | Move... ▾

From:	"Darryl Cole" <darryl@carfaxsecurity.com>
To:	"'raymond delauney'" <raymonddelauney@yahoo.co.uk>
Subject:	RE: Security work
Date:	Thu, 1 Dec 2005 17:24:15 -0000

Hello

We pay £12 per hour and it's Friday and Saturdays from 9.30 to 2.30 and I pay cash at the end of the shift on Saturday. Can you start work this Friday or Saturday?

Regards

END OF CORRESPONDENCE

DNA

| Delete | Reply ▾ | Forward ▾ | Spam | Move... ▾ |

Date:	Mon, 15 Jan 2007 18:40:56 +0000 (GMT)
From:	"raymond delauney" <raymonddelauney@yahoo.co.uk>
Subject:	DNA
To:	Sales@genetictruthtesting.com

Hi,

I just like to say well done on the unbelievable breakthroughs you've made on the discovery of DNA.

This incredible scientific advancement has been solely responsible for emptying the streets of criminals.

I'll get straight down to brass tacks:

I desperately need to save my marriage, and with your help I think I can.

My wife found a pair of knickers in the back seat of my car. She did not immediately identify them as hers. On the front of the garment is an ugly tree shaped beige stain.

Unfortunately the knickers do not belong to my wife, although after hours of rows, accusations and counter accusations I believe I have injected enough just enough doubt in her mind to suggest that they might be.

The offending underwear actually belongs to the babysitter (now sacked).

Where do I go from here?

Here's my plan:

I send the knickers registered delivery to you for DNA test along with a strand of hair from the wife's head. You then send me the underwear back with an official looking sticker on it saying something like: 'Item Processed DNA match consistent with hair strand belong to Mrs Ruth Delauney' (feel free to add any complicated scientific jargon you think may help).

I'd be extremely grateful for this. I'd be prepared to hand over some green backs to facilitate the procedure and cover costs – you'd also have the added satisfaction of saving my marriage.

I really need this as a divorce would ruin me financially and the kids would miss out at Xmas time.

Yours desperately,

Raymond Delauney

| Delete | Reply ▾ | Forward ▾ | Spam | Move... ▾ |

From:	Sales@genetictruthtesting.com
To:	"raymond delauney" <raymonddelauney@yahoo.co.uk>
Subject:	Re: DNA
Date:	Mon, 15 Jan 2007 13:02:17 -0600

Raymond,

The cost of the DNA extraction from the stained garment is $300.00. If it is successful, your wife's buccal swab collection and report is $160, which includes shipping in both directions. Hair is $80 more and we need 5–10 plucked hairs with the follicle (root).

Please let me know if I can be of further assistance.

Sincerely,

James Harborne
Genetic Truth Testing, Inc.
1800 Clear Bay Drive., Suite 667
Seabrook, TX 77586
888-874-9998
817-285-9998 x809
Fax: 800-899-4899
Sales@genetictruthtesting.com
www.genetictruthtesting.com

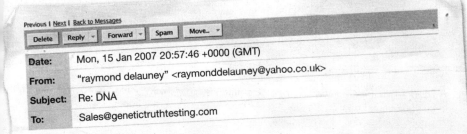

| Delete | Reply ▾ | Forward ▾ | Spam | Move... ▾ |

Date:	Mon, 15 Jan 2007 20:57:46 +0000 (GMT)
From:	"raymond delauney" <raymonddelauney@yahoo.co.uk>
Subject:	Re: DNA
To:	Sales@genetictruthtesting.com

James,

Sounds like a bargain.

Listen, I'll pay double your quote in sterling, say £450. BUT I need a result that says the knicker juice matches my missus (i.e. is consistent with the hair). Otherwise my marriage is well and truly over. Any other result will effectively see me facilitate and finance my own (very) expensive divorce.

I'll get a thatch of the wife's barnet, swathe it carefully inside her knickers and put some cling film round it to keep the freshness. I'll send it off to you tomorrow and mark it for your attention.

It's vital you and no one else handle my wife's knickers.

Make sure you attach some sort of fancy worded printout that puts me in the clear.

I'll need to ring you before it is sent because one mistake here could see me sleeping rough.

I DO NOT intend to pay half my salary to the old bat for the rest of my natural, not at my time of life.

What is a buccal swab, anyway?

Thanks,

I appreciate this, James.

Raymond

| Delete | Reply ▾ | Forward ▾ | Spam | Move... ▾ |

From:	Sales@genetictruthtesting.com
To:	"raymond delauney" <raymonddelauney@yahoo.co.uk>
Subject:	Re: DNA
Date:	Mon, 15 Jan 2007 15:49:13 -0600

Raymond,

We cannot provide a false report. We can only test what we receive and provide truthful results. No amount of money could ever change this.

James

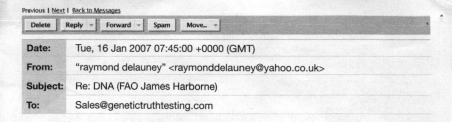

| Delete | Reply ⌄ | Forward ⌄ | Spam | Move... ⌄ |

Date:	Tue, 16 Jan 2007 07:45:00 +0000 (GMT)
From:	"raymond delauney" <raymonddelauney@yahoo.co.uk>
Subject:	Re: DNA (FAO James Harborne)
To:	Sales@genetictruthtesting.com

James,

This is very disappointing. I've never believed the misguided notion that honesty is the best policy. I work in the second hand car business and in my experience you often need to be a little economical with the truth to get the right results.

I've had a good think on the matter and have come up with the perfect solution to suit all parties.

I'll let the wife see me put the knickers in a package with her head hair and then go and pretend to post it. Once I'm in the car I'll re-open the package, remove the babysitter's knickers and substitute them for a pair belonging to the wife, one that I have removed from the laundry basket. That way you will be testing her knickers and therefore should get her DNA.

I'll also send a tissue containing a sperm sample of mine just in case any different varieties of jis are discovered on her underwear. The way she looks these days I very much doubt anyone has been in for a dip, but you never know.

My wife's knickers are navy blue and the babysitter's are white so DO NOT make any reference to the colour of the underwear in your report. There are no visible stains on the wife's panties, but I know she wears them for at least two days at a time so there should be some moistness on there to work with.

I appreciate this, James.

Let me have a full cost for the above and I'll release the funds to you immediately.

Best regards,

Raymond Delauney

Delete | Reply ⌄ | Forward ⌄ | Spam | Move... ⌄

From:	sales@genetictruthtesting.com
To:	"raymond delauney" <raymonddelauney@yahoo.co.uk>
Subject:	Re: DNA
Date:	Tue, 16 Jan 2007 06:58:07 -0600

A DNA extraction from an unknown stain is $300 and the hair and comparison report is $240 payable in US funds by credit card.

If you are present on her sample, the profile will be contaminated and a differential lysis will be required to separate the profile, which is $700.

Genetic Truth Testing centre prepares the clothing sample for extraction. There is no reference to the clothing item tested on the report. The lab will report that they received a microtube with cloth cuttings, however if you give her full access to the case she can call to discuss the tested article. We will not lie about what we received for testing to any person who has access to the complete file, which is provided by a unique order number we provide at the time of purchase. If you do not give her this order number, she cannot access the file.

The first process should begin with you ordering the test and then you send us the knickers and 10 of your wife's plucked hairs (with root).

Again, we must reiterate that we will not lie or make up data however, we will test any article received.

James

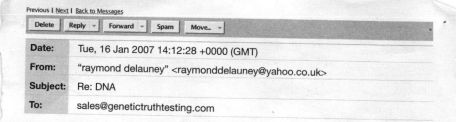

| Delete | Reply ▾ | Forward ▾ | Spam | Move... ▾ | |

Date:	Tue, 16 Jan 2007 14:12:28 +0000 (GMT)
From:	"raymond delauney" <raymonddelauney@yahoo.co.uk>
Subject:	Re: DNA
To:	sales@genetictruthtesting.com

James,

Quit throwing figures at me. I've got the readies, don't panic. I just need you to be ultra clear on a few minor but important details.

Another thing, I don't want to be present in the sample. I live in England so I'm hardly going to pay for the airfare to attend the examination! Thought you might have worked that one out.

Great news about there being no reference to clothes.

The way I see it there's no reason our knicker switch idea shouldn't work a treat.

Obviously I'll opt for the strictly no access option. I don't want the old bat babbling to anybody wearing a white coat – or else I'll be eating out of plastic plates for most of next week.

Just send me the order number and we can pretend there isn't one and that discussion isn't optional.

How about a cool $1,000 deposited in your bank account if you phone her to tell her the news yourself?

Do we have a taker? I think we do.

Some fancy dan American accent dropping in lots of scientific names and vouching for my innocence is what I need to put the cream on this cake.

I can't wait to rip out a bunch of her hair, root included.

Good work,

Raymond Delauney

25

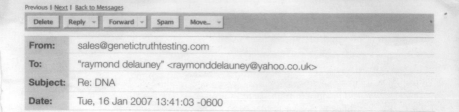

From:	sales@genetictruthtesting.com
To:	"raymond delauney" <raymonddelauney@yahoo.co.uk>
Subject:	Re: DNA
Date:	Tue, 16 Jan 2007 13:41:03 -0600

Raymond,

You being present in the sample means that we obtain your DNA due to semen/sperm.

We do not take bank or wire transfers because we are not authorized to disclose our account information. We take all credit/debit cards, paypal, or you can send a money order.

I am not authorized to call England and provide the results. You can have her call here and have her results read to her if she has the order number, however, you did not want her to have the order information.

We will do DNA extractions on anything but we will report only the truth of the DNA obtained from that sample. We cannot extend special favors and/or take additional money other then our actual charges.

Your order number is assigned by the purchase system when payment is obtained. If you are paying by credit card, please provide your complete billing address, credit card number, expiration date, and CVV number on the back of your card and I will complete your transaction. You can also order online at http://www.genetictruthtesting.com/samples.htm (select unknown sample and hair).

James

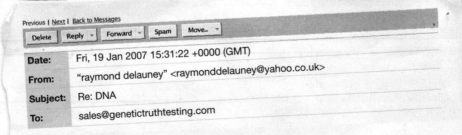

Date:	Fri, 19 Jan 2007 15:31:22 +0000 (GMT)
From:	"raymond delauney" <raymonddelauney@yahoo.co.uk>
Subject:	Re: DNA
To:	sales@genetictruthtesting.com

James,

I need a huge favour. I can't really afford the wait in sending off the knickers. The old bat is threatening to chuck me out tonight.

Change of plan:

Send me back a mail from your email address. Cut and paste the following information and insert it in the mail to me.

****

Hello Mr Delauney,

Thanks you for your mail.

Of course we would like to help you, however the process could be longthy and expensive.

If, as you say, your wife is dark haired and the baby sitter blonde then you are better off taking this simple but effective test.

Pour a generous amount of household vinegar over the affected area of the knickers. If you have slept with a blonde haired woman the solution will turn blue.

This is due to an over presence of white blood cells reacting with blonder, lighter cells.

If the knickers belong to your darker haired wife then there will be no reaction. This test is 100% reliable.

Best regards,

James Harborne
Chicf Scientist
Genetic Truth Testing, Inc.
1800 Clear Bay Drive., Suite 667
Seabrook, TX 77586
888-874-9998
817-285-9998 x809
Fax: 800-899-4899
Sales@genetictruthtesting.com
www. genetictruthtesting.com

****

I really appreciate this, James.

I'll make it worth your while.

Please reply immediately to help save my marriage.

Raymond

Previous I Next I Back to Messages

| Delete | Reply ▼ | Forward ▼ | Spam | Move... ▼ |

From:	sales@genetictruthtesting.com
To:	"raymond delauney" <raymonddelauney@yahoo.co.uk>
Subject:	Re: DNA
Date:	Fri, 19 Jan 2007 10:18:23 -0600

Raymond,

I wish I could help you but we are not permitted to fabricate anything.

James

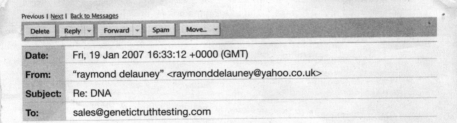

Previous I Next I Back to Messages

| Delete | Reply ▼ | Forward ▼ | Spam | Move... ▼ |

Date:	Fri, 19 Jan 2007 16:33:12 +0000 (GMT)
From:	"raymond delauney" <raymonddelauney@yahoo.co.uk>
Subject:	Re: DNA
To:	sales@genetictruthtesting.com

James,

I'm begging you buddy.

I'm literally typing this on my knees.

You wouldn't be fabricating anything – merely cutting and pasting my mail.

You'd save my marriage and get $10,000 big ones.

Yeah, that's right.

The old vinegar trick should do the business. She'd never question anything from a top scientist like you.

No one would be any the wiser and you'd have 10 large to spend on hookers, down the casino or on whatever you want.

Please do it for me, Jamesie.

I need it done, ideally in the next half hour.

Thanks

Ray

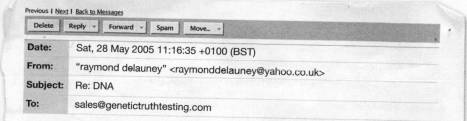

Date:	Sat, 28 May 2005 11:16:35 +0100 (BST)
From:	"raymond delauney" <raymonddelauney@yahoo.co.uk>
Subject:	Re: DNA
To:	sales@genetictruthtesting.com

Ray,

I wish I could help but I would never jeopardize my job and position by sending such a false statement.

James

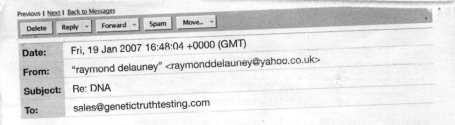

Date:	Fri, 19 Jan 2007 16:48:04 +0000 (GMT)
From:	"raymond delauney" <raymonddelauney@yahoo.co.uk>
Subject:	Re: DNA
To:	sales@genetictruthtesting.com

Okay James,

I understand, I'll use your details and forge something myself. I'm sorry but I have to protect myself against huge alimony payments.

She definitely won't contact you but if she does please let me know immediately and I'll get a friend to ring her up using an American accent.

You've been great about this. I owe you one. If you ever visit London I'll sort you out free hire of our top of the range BMW series for as long as your stay.

Thanks,

Raymond

From:	sales@genetictruthtesting.com
To:	"raymond delauney" <raymonddelauney@yahoo.co.uk>
Subject:	Re: DNA
Date:	Fri, 19 Jan 2007 13:21:02 -0600

Thanks Raymond, glad you understand. Good luck with your situation.

James

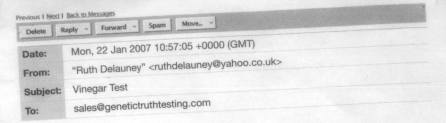

Date:	Mon, 22 Jan 2007 10:57:05 +0000 (GMT)
From:	"Ruth Delauney" <ruthdelauney@yahoo.co.uk>
Subject:	Vinegar Test
To:	sales@genetictruthtesting.com

Hello,

I trust this finds you in good health.

My husband and I have conducted the 'vinegar test' on the pair of knickers and the result is negative.

I find this remarkable, as I am CERTAIN the garment in question does not belong to me. It's far too tight for me, in a colour I never wear and the label is from a shop I have never visited.

Either I am going mad or there's something seriously suspicious here.

My friend Silvia, whose husband is a pharmacist, has never heard of the vinegar test. Is it medically proven and always 100% successful?

Best wishes,

Ruth Delauney

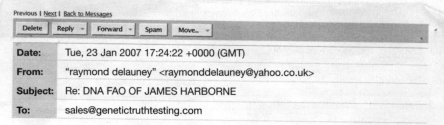

Date:	Tue, 23 Jan 2007 17:24:22 +0000 (GMT)
From:	"raymond delauney" <raymonddelauney@yahoo.co.uk>
Subject:	Re: DNA FAO OF JAMES HARBORNE
To:	sales@genetictruthtesting.com

James,

I believe my wife may have contacted you. I'm sorry, she may have seen some notes I deliberately left out for her to see.

I printed out a mail from myself advising the vinegar test and then superimposed your email address and photocopied it to look like you had sent me a mail advising it.

If she has contacted you or does so in the future just assure her the test is 100% reliable and then I'll wrap it up from there. I think the dumb ass has bought it so we should be in the clear.

Nice one,

Ray

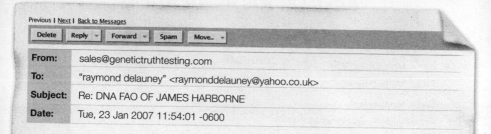

Delete | Reply | Forward | Spam | Move...

From:	sales@genetictruthtesting.com
To:	"raymond delauney" <raymonddelauney@yahoo.co.uk>
Subject:	Re: DNA FAO OF JAMES HARBORNE
Date:	Tue, 23 Jan 2007 11:54:01 -0600

I received an email from her and there will be no response.

That's the best I can do.

James

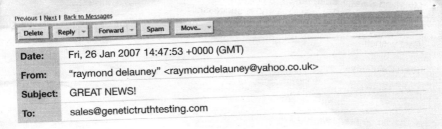

Delete | Reply | Forward | Spam | Move...

Date:	Fri, 26 Jan 2007 14:47:53 +0000 (GMT)
From:	"raymond delauney" <raymonddelauney@yahoo.co.uk>
Subject:	GREAT NEWS!
To:	sales@genetictruthtesting.com

James,

I've just found out a good friend mate slept with my missus 7 years ago!!!

There was she giving it the holier than thou when she was being rammed by my pal!

He confessed last night after we got absolutely blotto on all day session down the Blue Duck. He was embarrassed about it. He should be embarrassed! I'm the schmuk who married her!

I was so happy I could have kissed him. Instead I let him off the last year's payments on the Nissan Micra I sold him last year.

This makes the panty argument irrelevant, although I see no point in putting my hands up to it. May as well claim the moral wasteland.

Thanks for all your help, buddy.

Raymond

END OF CORRESPONDENCE

31

ADVISOR JOB APPLICATION

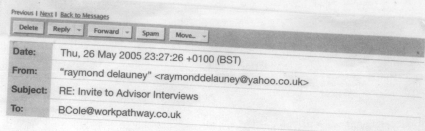

Date: Thu, 26 May 2005 23:27:26 +0100 (BST)

From: "raymond delauney" <raymonddelauney@yahoo.co.uk>

Subject: RE: Invite to Advisor Interviews

To: BCole@workpathway.co.uk

Hi,

I had a chat to some colleagues and they agreed I would make a good candidate for the position advertised. I would, therefore, like to confirm my interest in the position of 'advisor'. I suppose you could say I was advised to go for the position of advisor!

I have attached the completed questionnaire and look forward to delivering my 'greatest risk' speech on Tuesday. I have been practising and am expecting a standing ovation!

Relentlessly,

Raymond Delauney

Subject: RE: Invite to Advisor Interviews

Date: Fri, 27 May 2005 10:13:34 +0100

From: "Beth Cole" <BCole@workpathway.co.uk>

To: "raymond delauney" <raymonddelauney@yahoo.co.uk>

Dear Raymond,

Thank you for getting back to me, unfortunately I am sorry to say that we do not have any interview spaces left as they were due to availability.

We are going to be constantly recruiting through out the year, so we will put you forward for the next round of interviews.

Kind regards

Beth

Beth Cole
HR Executive

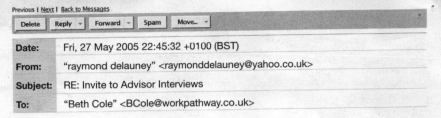

Date:	Fri, 27 May 2005 22:45:32 +0100 (BST)
From:	"raymond delauney" <raymonddelauney@yahoo.co.uk>
Subject:	RE: Invite to Advisor Interviews
To:	"Beth Cole" <BCole@workpathway.co.uk>

Beth,

What are you playing at, sister?

Do you know what you've just done?

You've almost deprived the company you work for of their prize asset – me.

I say 'almost' because I flatly refuse to accept your rejection.

Mistakes are made, some oaf failed to sign up the Beatles, some dunderhead signed up Michelle McManus. Don't be an oaf, Beth. I won't bring this up with your superior officers – this time.

Let me know when you can re-schedule me for the interview and you'll hear no more of your latest gaffe. I've been practising my speech in front of the mirror and, frankly, it's damned good.

I spent time filling out the form, which you didn't even bother reading. If you had you might have realised I have a whole lot of class which your company would benefit from.

And another thing, no offence, but you really should lose that poncey signature of yours.

Relentlessly,

Raymond

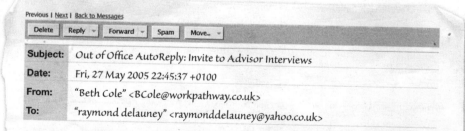

Subject:	Out of Office AutoReply: Invite to Advisor Interviews
Date:	Fri, 27 May 2005 22:45:37 +0100
From:	"Beth Cole" <BCole@workpathway.co.uk>
To:	"raymond delauney" <raymonddelauney@yahoo.co.uk>

I am out of the office until the 13th April 2005. Should you require any assistance please contact Karen Upson on 0207 393 9000

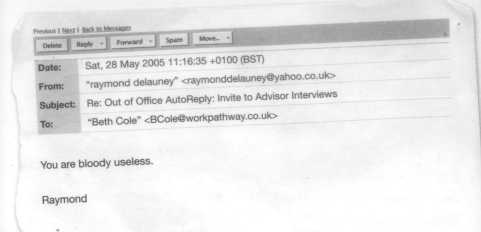

| Delete | Reply ▾ | Forward ▾ | Spam | Move... ▾ |

Date:	Sat, 28 May 2005 11:16:35 +0100 (BST)
From:	"raymond delauney" <raymonddelauney@yahoo.co.uk>
Subject:	Re: Out of Office AutoReply: Invite to Advisor Interviews
To:	"Beth Cole" <BCole@workpathway.co.uk>

You are bloody useless.

Raymond

SOME MONTHS LATER

| Delete | Reply ▾ | Forward ▾ | Spam | Move... ▾ |

Date:	Sun, 24 Jul 2005 01:51:18 +0100 (BST)
From:	"raymond delauney" <raymonddelauney@yahoo.co.uk>
Subject:	Interview Date
To:	BCole@workpathway.co.uk

Hello Beth,

One hopes that this mail finds you in a satisfactory condition.

I should like to confirm that I can and will be attending your next batch of interviews.

There was an administrative mix up with my first application, which resulted in my non-appearance. Fortunately my diary has now been freed up sufficiently to allow me visitation.

When and where do you want to slot me in?

I'll need to know as soon as is possible so as to get my suit in the dry cleaners. On Tuesdays Suit Chute do two items for £6 so if you could let me know by then it'd be greatly appreciated.

I have attached the questionnaire and have prepared myself fully for interaction.

Best,

Raymond Delauney

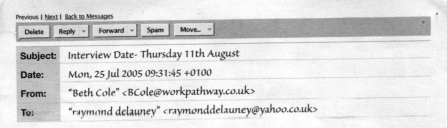

| Delete | Reply ▾ | Forward ▾ | Spam | Move... ▾ |

Subject:	Interview Date- Thursday 11th August
Date:	Mon, 25 Jul 2005 09:31:45 +0100
From:	"Beth Cole" <BCole@workpathway.co.uk>
To:	"raymond delauney" <raymonddelauney@yahoo.co.uk>

Dear Raymond,

Thank you for your email expressing your interest in attending an interview day for the advisor position.

I have placed you in the interview day on Thursday 11th August 2005; please can you bring along with you the question preparation sheet.

If you have any questions about the day please do not hesitate to contact me on 0207 961 0774.

We look forward to meeting you on the day.

Kind regards

Beth

Beth Cole
HR Executive

Date:	Wed, 27 Jul 2005 23:09:19 +0100 (BST)
From:	"raymond delauney" <raymonddelauney@yahoo.co.uk>
Subject:	Re: Interview Date- Thursday 11th August
To:	"Beth Cole" <BCole@workpathway.co.uk>

Beth,

Good girl.

I'll need to know how much you guys are willing to pay me before I make any declarations of intent – ballpark at least.

If you want the best – you gotta pay for it.

If you like, I could assist with the training and help decide who makes the cut and who should be on the next stage outta town.

I'm an excellent judge of character.

Could you also list all the perks associated with the job such as hols, pension, gym membership etc.

Thanks,

Raymond

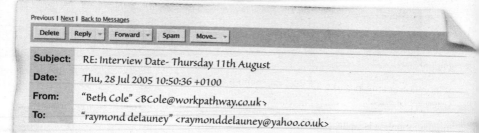

Subject:	RE: Interview Date- Thursday 11th August
Date:	Thu, 28 Jul 2005 10:50:36 +0100
From:	"Beth Cole" <BCole@workpathway.co.uk>
To:	"raymond delauney" <raymonddelauney@yahoo.co.uk>

Dear Raymond,

The salary for an advisor within London is 27,500.

You get 25 days holiday a year and you can start contributing to your pension after three months with the company, after 6 months the company will start double matching your contribution up to 8%.

Please could you let me know soon whether you would like to attend an assessment day as spaces are limited.

If you do wish to attend an interview could I kindly ask that you re-attach your application and send it through to me via email so we have an electronic version of it.

Kind regards

Beth

Beth Cole
HR Executive

| Delete | Reply ▾ | Forward ▾ | Spam | Move... ▾ |

Date:	Thu, 28 Jul 2005 16:11:00 +0100 (BST)
From:	"raymond delauney" <raymonddelauney@yahoo.co.uk>
Subject:	RE: Interview Date- Thursday 11th August
To:	"Beth Cole" <BCole@workpathway.co.uk>

Listen Beth,

Everything seems in order. It'll take a minimum of £30k to capture my services. That will be money well spent.

If everyone else is yelling £27k I think I'm worth £30k as I'll be taking the lead.

Once you get this rubber stamped I'll send through my application again.

See you on the 11th.

Regards,

Raymond

Delete | Reply ▾ | Forward ▾ | Spam | Move.. ▾

Subject:	RE: Interview Date- Thursday 11th August
Date:	Thu, 28 Jul 2005 18:06:09 +0100
From:	"Beth Cole" <BCole@workpathway.co.uk>
To:	"raymond delauney" <raymonddelauney@yahoo.co.uk>

Dear Raymond

This position has been advertised at £27,500 only and this salary is not negotiable.

If you therefore feel that this salary is inappropriate, please could you let me know by 10:00am tomorrow otherwise we will assume you do not wish to take your application any further.

Yours sincerely

Beth

Beth Cole
HR Executive

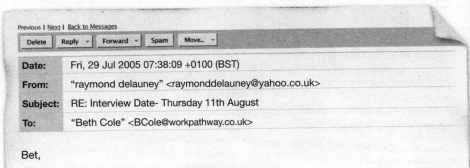

Delete | Reply ▾ | Forward ▾ | Spam | Move.. ▾

Date:	Fri, 29 Jul 2005 07:38:09 +0100 (BST)
From:	"raymond delauney" <raymonddelauney@yahoo.co.uk>
Subject:	RE: Interview Date- Thursday 11th August
To:	"Beth Cole" <BCole@workpathway.co.uk>

Bet,

You're being a little bit stubborn here.

I'll bank the £27,500 opening gambit and then work on getting a raise when I'm firmly ensconced – shouldn't be too difficult once you see what I've got to offer.

I've attached the application form once again.

Raymond

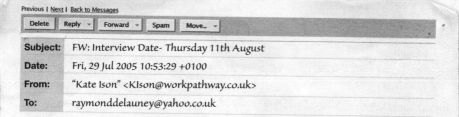

Subject:	FW: Interview Date- Thursday 11th August
Date:	Fri, 29 Jul 2005 10:53:29 +0100
From:	"Kate Ison" <KIson@workpathway.co.uk>
To:	raymonddelauney@yahoo.co.uk

Dear Raymond

Following your recent emails to my colleague Beth, I am writing to advise you that we shall be withdrawing your application. This decision has been based on your correspondence with us, which has shown both lack of professionalism and respect.

Yours sincerely

Katie Ison

HR Officer
WorkPathway UK Ltd

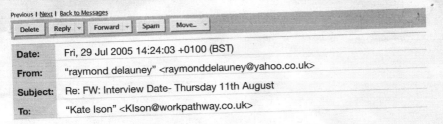

Date:	Fri, 29 Jul 2005 14:24:03 +0100 (BST)
From:	"raymond delauney" <raymonddelauney@yahoo.co.uk>
Subject:	Re: FW: Interview Date- Thursday 11th August
To:	"Kate Ison" <KIson@workpathway.co.uk>

Ison,

Firstly, I'm not sure you can legally withdraw my interview application at this late stage. I have already booked a day's holiday at work so I'd need to be recompensed for it if this was indeed the case. I was, in fact, quite terse with the woman at HR in booking the day off, which resulted in me receiving a second written warning. So, inadvertently I think as this happened as a consequence of my interview date, you should understandably bear some responsibility.

Secondly, I cannot recall an instance where I was either disrespectful or unprofessional to your colleague Beth. It is possible that she is unused to dealing with clients on a directorial level and so felt uneasy in any communication with me. I'm more than prepared to overlook this matter.

I think the best course of action at this juncture in time is to be adult about this and just proceed with the interview on the original date.

I rate myself as a superb acquisition. I am extremely confident in my abilities and this is born out of knowing what I am capable of. It would be foolish of you on your part not to recognise this.

Get back to me with confirmation of the interview date and we'll say no more of the matter.

Raymond Delauney

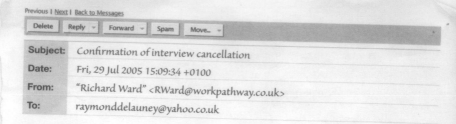

Subject:	Confirmation of interview cancellation
Date:	Fri, 29 Jul 2005 15:09:34 +0100
From:	"Richard Ward" <RWard@workpathway.co.uk>
To:	raymonddelauney@yahoo.co.uk

Mr Delauney,

I apologise for any inconvenience caused but am afraid that I am writing to confirm that we will not be inviting you to interview for a position with us.

I have read through all your correspondence with my HR colleagues and I fully support their decision. It is clear from your communication that you would not be happy in this organisation and would not be comfortable in the role of one of our advisors. It would not be a good use of your time or ours to include you in one of our selection days.

With best wishes,

Richard

Richard Ward
Chief Executive Officer

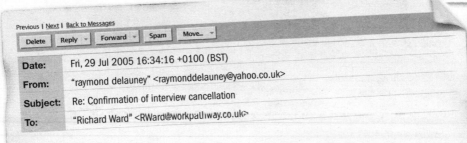

Date:	Fri, 29 Jul 2005 16:34:16 +0100 (BST)
From:	"raymond delauney" <raymonddelauney@yahoo.co.uk>
Subject:	Re: Confirmation of interview cancellation
To:	"Richard Ward" <RWard@workpathway.co.uk>

Rich,

At last I seem to be speaking to someone with a degree of authority and an ounce of intelligence.

I've often found the higher up you go – the nicer the people are.

I don't know what the girl snitches who work below you have invented but as far as I can tell I've done nothing wrong apart from apply for a position with your company that I believe suits my skills well.

All I want is a chance to demonstrate this to you in person – is that too much to ask?

I am a good worker, Richard, bloody good.

If for whatever bizarre reason you still wish to blacklist me from an interview then that is your prerogative. But I'll need £70, which is what I am normally paid at work. I've booked a day off and thoroughly upset the overweight vegetarian girl who runs HR in the process. I'll be candid here, that girl thoroughly detests me and would like nothing better than to see me leave.

And now, seemingly I've booked a day off to no avail. It really makes my blood boil.

Allow me to turn up. Sometime you've got to go with your gut instinct on these things. Throw me in the mix and let me do the rest. I have spent a couple of hours rehearsing my 'risk' speech. It's sharp, Richard, and has a punchy finish.

Get back to me before close of business today as I'll need to plan my week ahead.

Thanks,
Raymond Delauney

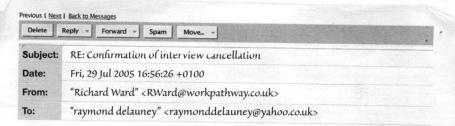

Previous I Next I Back to Messages

| Delete | Reply ⌄ | Forward ⌄ | Spam | Move... ⌄ |

Subject:	RE: Confirmation of interview cancellation
Date:	Fri, 29 Jul 2005 16:56:26 +0100
From:	"Richard Ward" <RWard@workpathway.co.uk>
To:	"raymond delauney" <raymonddelauney@yahoo.co.uk>

I can only repeat the message of my earlier email. I'm sorry but this is not the organisation for you.

I am sorry for any inconvenience this may have caused but we will not be paying any compensation.

I understand that this is not the outcome you hoped for but there will be no point in communicating with us further regarding this decision.

Richard Ward

Chief Executive Officer

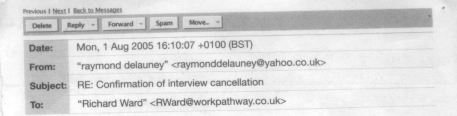

Date:	Mon, 1 Aug 2005 16:10:07 +0100 (BST)
Delete Reply Forward Spam Move...	
From:	"raymond delauney" <raymonddelauney@yahoo.co.uk>
Subject:	RE: Confirmation of interview cancellation
To:	"Richard Ward" <RWard@workpathway.co.uk>

Rich,

I trust you enjoyed a pleasant weekend.

I didn't.

I really don't think we should rush into any rash decisions here. If I were granted an interview I would really give it my all.

For your information I was dismissed from my former job late on Friday evening. The row I had last week with one obese vegetarian dimwit escalated into a full-scale incident, which led to me being hauled in front of the MD.

Officially it was my third strike though I still maintain it was only my second written warning. I didn't dispute the fact that I received two verbal warnings in my first month but thought that was in the dim and distant past and should not be held against me – since then my conduct has been exemplary.

After eloquently presenting my case for ten minutes I began to realise my words of wisdom were falling on deaf ears and an irreversible decision had already been arrived at.

Nothing I said was going to make him change his mind so I contented myself by ferociously insulting him and turning his desk over as I made my exit. In hindsight that might not have been a good idea as I'm still owed three weeks' wages.

I'm now without a job or income so I would genuinely appreciate an interview right now.

How about I just turn up at the interview, nothing is said about the water that has already passed under the bridge and you just take a look at what I've got? Makes sense to me.

If an interview is granted I obviously will not take any legal action against you, even if I'm not successful with the interview and my application goes no further.

Give it a thought, as I really need a break here.

I've got a feeling that things could turn out well for all parties concerned. Every cloud has a silver lining.

Best regards,

Raymond Delauney

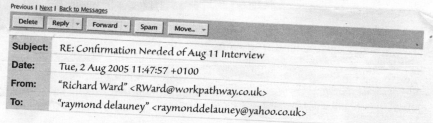

Delete   Reply ▾   Forward ▾   Spam   Move... ▾

Subject:	RE: Confirmation Needed of Aug 11 Interview
Date:	Tue, 2 Aug 2005 11:47:57 +0100
From:	"Richard Ward" <RWard@workpathway.co.uk>
To:	"raymond delauney" <raymonddelauney@yahoo.co.uk>

Mr Delauney,

I received your email yesterday.

I can confirm that we do NOT wish you to attend an interview at Work Pathway and that this is the last communication, which you will receive from us.

I am sorry this has not worked out and I wish you all the best in your search for work elsewhere.

Richard

Richard Ward
Chief Executive Officer

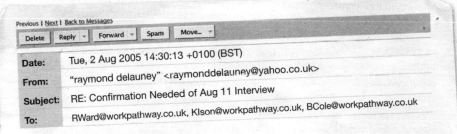

Delete   Reply ▾   Forward ▾   Spam   Move... ▾

Date:	Tue, 2 Aug 2005 14:30:13 +0100 (BST)
From:	"raymond delauney" <raymonddelauney@yahoo.co.uk>
Subject:	RE: Confirmation Needed of Aug 11 Interview
To:	RWard@workpathway.co.uk, KIson@workpathway.co.uk, BCole@workpathway.co.uk

Ward,

You and that ramshackle outfit you head up are nothing more than a bunch of messers.

Before I applied for a job with you I already had work, now, directly as a result of communicating with you and your bunch of crony blockheads, I am jobless and potless.

Thanks very much.

You Oaf.

Regards

Raymond Delauney

NO REPLY

43

QUESTIONNAIRE

You will participate in a group training session to facilitate: diversity awareness, building rapport, conflict management and creating a work context that allows you to operate at your best. You will be spending a half day with us during your interview process to allow you to sample the kind of training attitudes, values and behaviours that are current in WorkPathway.

Please answer the questions honestly, we are more interested in your accurate self-awareness than in the content of your answer. Bring a copy of your answer to the interview with you.

Name:

When operating/working at your best you are like what? What is a metaphor that represents you working really well?
(*Past examples have been: a 12 armed octopus, a train on slick tracks, float like a butterfly, sting like a bee, a butterfly that can visit lots of flowers and knows its hedgerow boundaries.*)

I'm like a swan, graceful on the outside but paddling furiously underneath. This comparison is especially apt for me because the toes on my left foot are webbed. At first this embarrassed me but now I've come to accept myself as unique.

A perfect team for you, in which you can work at your best, is like what?
(*Past examples have been, a boat crew where we recognise each other's strengths and change leaders according to the weather conditions, a good cake where the individual ingredients get changed in the mix, a banquet in which everybody brings their speciality dishes and one person co-ordinates how it is presented, a gymnastics team where we compete individually but for one country.*)

I like to work together with a team — side by side. I'll work with them in the trenches, bayonet to bayonet or from behind the scenes, planning moves, strategies, tactics and techniques. Like a team we'll live by the sword — or die on it.

You can natter all you like about working but in my experience every team needs a skipper. A chief, a head, a boss, a captain. Call him what you will — you bloody well need one. I'm talking about someone who leads and is followed. Someone who is decisive when all around are uncertain. Someone to grab the game by the scruff of the neck the way Stevie Gerrard did when his team trailed in 3-0. A Francis Drake who had the composure to finish his game of bowls before he minced all those Spaniards.

I see myself as a leader; I'll speak any language that gets me results whether it is industrial, directorial or plain bloody common sense. I expect to have a major impact on your company when selected.

Position: **DEPUTY NIGHT EDITOR**

Mercury is THE newspaper phenomenon of the past five years.

It has established an enviable reputation as the first source of news for millions of commuters in dozens of cities across Britain.

We are looking for a first-class editorial operator who knows how to write accurate, brilliant, punchy news stories, sparkling headlines and is a wizard with QuarkXPress.

You will already be on the back or middle bench of another national newspaper or on a major regional daily newspaper. We have a small team and tight deadlines which means you must not be afraid of hard work and the pressure of delivering a top-quality product day after day.

We will fashion the job to suit your skills but it will probably involve revising, subbing and designing news pages as well as taking charge of late editions of the paper.

Your reward will be a competitive salary and a chance to work on a successful newspaper which is changing the face of the industry.

Please send your CV to John Livingstone at the address below.

Alternatively, send email: john.livingstone@mercuryrising.co.uk

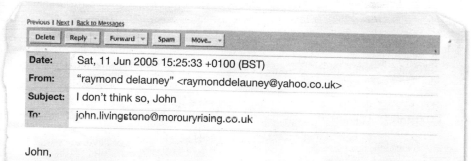

Previous | Next | Back to Messages

Delete	Reply	Forward	Spam	Move...

Date:	Sat, 11 Jun 2005 15:25:33 +0100 (BST)
From:	"raymond delauney" <raymonddelauney@yahoo.co.uk>
Subject:	I don't think so, John
To:	john.livingstone@morouryrising.co.uk

John,

Thanks for contacting me about the vacant position of DEPUTY NIGHT EDITOR.

Unfortunately I am not interested in the position at this moment in time and, to be perfectly frank, I never will be.

I have been with the Mail for four years and during this time have been happy to work here. I find it odd that anyone would think I would want to take a hefty pay cut, work nights and become your deputy.

I hope you don't take umbrage but I feel the Mercury is somewhat beneath my station in terms of what I've achieved in journalism. You wouldn't expect Shakespeare to write a Carry On script and similarly I wouldn't pen for the Mercury. Congratulations on the pricing policy of the rag you churn out – you've got it just about spot on.

I would be grateful if you do not approach me with a new improved offer – you'd only be wasting your time and mine. Find yourself another tea boy.

I understand you want the best in the business – and I am that – but loyalty is something money can't buy.

P.S. You might want to get a sub to check out your sloppy ad.

Regards,

Raymond Delauney

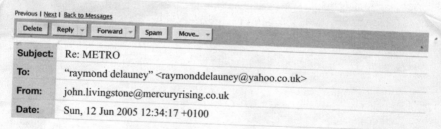

Delete | Reply ▾ | Forward ▾ | Spam | Move… ▾

Subject:	Re: METRO
To:	"raymond delauney" <raymonddelauney@yahoo.co.uk>
From:	john.livingstone@mercuryrising.co.uk
Date:	Sun, 12 Jun 2005 12:34:17 +0100

Dear Raymond,

Thank you for your email... given that I have never heard of you nor emailed you, I was surprised to receive a reply.

That said, I am exceedingly grateful you do not wish to join Mercury. Maybe when you have grown up a bit and stop sending ill-informed, petty-minded and insulting emails to people you do not know, I might consider you suitable for a position (probably some way beneath tea boy, however). In the mean time, enjoy your well-paid, extremely comfortable job on The Mail and I hope one day you manage to break into proper journalism.

Regards

John Livingstone

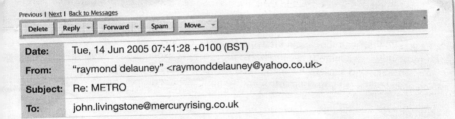

Date:	Tue, 14 Jun 2005 07:41:28 +0100 (BST)
From:	"raymond delauney" <raymonddelauney@yahoo.co.uk>
Subject:	Re: METRO
To:	john.livingstone@mercuryrising.co.uk

Oh, that's good Livingstone, awfully good.

First you send me a toadying mail practically begging me to join your ramshackle, two bob outfit. A missive so slimy, so sycophantic I can practically see your slobber all over it. And then, a mere two days later, directly after I've dismissed your job offer I've somewhat sourly been downgraded to a position some way 'beneath tea boy'.

Don't flatter yourself old chap, you make your own char. And I dare say your occupation necessitates a fair and steady swill. Doubtless to pull you through those elongated, tedious nights unloading bundles of newspaper from the back of lorries, swapping idle chatter in broken English (yours) with drivers from the backwaters of Eastern Europe.

I'd wager Sir, that the position you occupy is nothing more than that of a glorified security guard, the deluded species who, once handed a uniform, deem themselves to be a fundamental hinge of the secret service.

When I mentioned I work for the Mail I was referring to the Daily Mail and not, for example, the Hull and East Riding Mail. Most neutral observers would judge this journal to hold a little more in the way of prestige than the Mercury, the rag that serves only to litter the streets. If this leaflet were priced at tuppence you'd sell five copies a day.

If I were to upset my bosses at Associated Newspapers sufficiently well, and I'm thinking I might have to be responsible for at least one death here, then I may tumble far enough down the ladder to land a position as your boss. At which point you could watch me slurp the tea you make me as I supervise your loading/unloading lorries.

I'd be eternally grateful if you didn't inconvenience me again with any further correspondence. I must confess you are really beginning to irk me.

Regards,

Raymond Delauney

NO REPLY

DOG GROOMER JOB APPLICATION

Grooming parlour requires a dog groomer for immediate start. Must speak good standard of English, have visa to work in UK and have five year's experience. Lovely working environment.

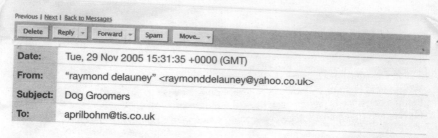

Previous | Next | Back to Messages

| Delete | Reply ▾ | Forward ▾ | Spam | Move... ▾ |

Date:	Tue, 29 Nov 2005 15:31:35 +0000 (GMT)
From:	"raymond delauney" <raymonddelauney@yahoo.co.uk>
Subject:	Dog Groomers
To:	aprilbohm@tis.co.uk

Hi,

I saw the ad above.

I am very interested in this job.

I love dogs with a passion, such loyal creatures.

I would be interested in grooming them. I have plenty of experience, mainly with Jack Russells. I have also groomed my own.

How much we talking?

Raymond

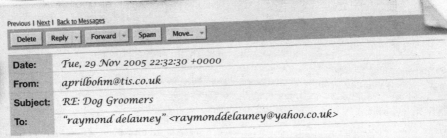

Previous | Next | Back to Messages

| Delete | Reply ▾ | Forward ▾ | Spam | Move... ▾ |

Date:	Tue, 29 Nov 2005 22:32:30 +0000
From:	aprilbohm@tis.co.uk
Subject:	RE: Dog Groomers
To:	"raymond delauney" <raymonddelauney@yahoo.co.uk>

Hi Raymond,

Thank you for your reply. Jack Russells are beautiful dogs but probably the easiest to groom. My clients have Bichons, Poodles, Cockers, Westies etc. Have you ever groomed any of these and what are your specialist cuts? I require a little more info. Where are you from and have you a permit to work in UK? (If appropriate.) How many years have you been grooming? Have you any qualifications?

Regards, April Bohm

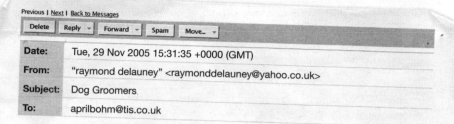

Delete   Reply ▾   Forward ▾   Spam   Move... ▾

Date:	Tue, 29 Nov 2005 15:31:35 +0000 (GMT)
From:	"raymond delauney" <raymonddelauney@yahoo.co.uk>
Subject:	Dog Groomers
To:	aprilbohm@tis.co.uk

Hi April,

I think you may have misunderstood me slightly.

When I said I had groomed Jack Russell's dogs I meant I had groomed my father's friend's dogs. He is named Jack Russell.

He has two mongrels that are non-pedigree but have a bit of Dachshund in them.

I have never heard of Bichons or Westies. I'm great with dogs and would like to work with them very much. I could take them for walks.

I thought you meant groom them to become better dogs rather than cut their hair. Still, I'm more than prepared to do that as well. I can be trained on the job, if you like.

Fear not, I'm British through and through. I can work anywhere you want me to. When would you want me to start?

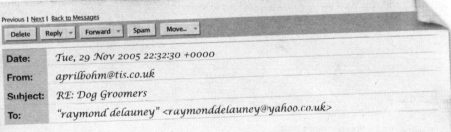

Delete   Reply ▾   Forward ▾   Spam   Move... ▾

Date:	Tue, 29 Nov 2005 22:32:30 +0000
From:	aprilbohm@tis.co.uk
Subject:	RE: Dog Groomers
To:	"raymond delauney" <raymonddelauney@yahoo.co.uk>

Hi Raymond,

Thank you for the information. The person I am looking for needs to have 5 years grooming experience as stated in the advert. The right person will also require knowledge of specialist breeds and cuts. I will hold your details on file for the future, however, you do not have the skills I require at the moment. Thank you for replying to the advert.

Regards, April Bohm

49

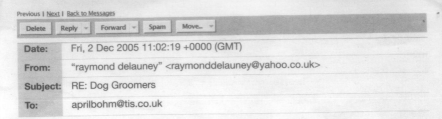

April,

My then, someone's got an overblown view of what it takes to clip a dog's barnet.
Leave the attitude in the kennel, sister.
I've sheared dogs plenty of times before and never received one complaint from any
of them.
Are you seriously suggesting it requires the same amount of training (five years) to
ponce around in a poodle parlour as it does to become a dentist, accountant or junior
rocket scientist?

Here's a question for you: Are you utterly insane?
You uncaringly state 'I do not have the skills you require, however you will hold my
details on file.' In case of what? An outbreak of plague affecting experienced dog
groomers?

Why is everyone sticking my name on files that no one ever refers to again? I must be
on more files than fingernails – and still nothing ever comes my way.
I had high hopes on this one. Do you know how demoralising it is to be told you ain't
smart enough to look after dogs?
Even that thick character on Coronation Street is an accomplished dog groomer. Was
it your intention to raise my sunken spirits only to pull the lead at the last minute?

Congratulations. You've made me feel really miserable. Looks like another crummy
Christmas for me.

Thanks a bunch

Raymond Delauney

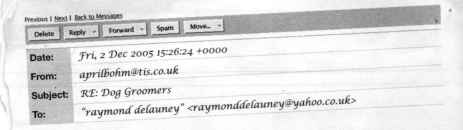

You kill me man.

50

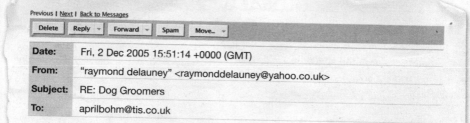

Date:	Fri, 2 Dec 2005 15:51:14 +0000 (GMT)
From:	"raymond delauney" <raymonddelauney@yahoo.co.uk>
Subject:	RE: Dog Groomers
To:	aprilbohm@tis.co.uk

'You kill me man.'

Is that all you've got to say after practically ruining my entire life?

I could go one of three ways about this.

1. Go to night school for five long years, take an HND in dog grooming and apply again with a little more confidence around Xmas time 2010.
2. Go to Never Never Land and wait for you to look me up on 'your file'.
3. Gain some crumb of satisfaction by sending you an insulting mail.

Yes, you guessed it. I've plumped for option 3.

I'll be poor again this Xmas. I thought this year might be different. The only way I can afford tinsel is if father sneezes.

Stick to handling dogs, lady. You ain't too good with people.

Raymond Delauney

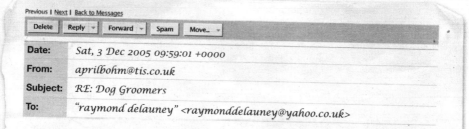

Date:	Sat, 3 Dec 2005 09:59:01 +0000
From:	aprilbohm@tis.co.uk
Subject:	RE: Dog Groomers
To:	"raymond delauney" <raymonddelauney@yahoo.co.uk>

It's very simple – you ain't the person for the job and I will delete your details "from file".

DO NOT EMAIL ME AGAIN

END OF CORRESPONDENCE

GLOBAL WARMING

To an American scientist with his own website and blog preaching about the dangers of global warming.

Delete   Reply ⌄   Forward ⌄   Spam   Move... ⌄

Date:	Wed, 1 Nov 2006 17:51:28 +0000 (GMT)
From:	"raymond delauney" <raymonddelauney@yahoo.co.uk>
Subject:	Global warming
To:	gerryzennon@savethegreenball.net

Hello,

My 8-year-old daughter has just come running to me in a flood of tears.

Why?

Because she thinks the world is going to end sometime soon and it's the fault of me and, to a lesser extent, my generation.

That's why.

Why does she think that? Because she takes it for gospel that overbearing boffins like you know more than ordinary folk like me.

Does it make you feel good? Making an eight-year-old girl with a mouth brace bawl her little eyes out?

Centuries ago wasn't it scientists who were worshipping the sun as a God?

Wasn't it scientists who thought the world was flat?

And wasn't it a scientist who invented the nuclear bomb?

Hell, before Newton came along not one single scientist could work out what gravity was.

I'm a salesman, have been for 20 years. Think you guys are smarter than me, do you?

Listen, I sell to put food on the table. Give me some shit and I'll sell it.

If I don't sell I get fired. Simple as that. The pressure is on me every week. Yet, the wife has a direct debit with you scientists at the cancer charity and I'll confess it rankles with me.

Every day you scientists go to work in your white coats and fiddle about with a few test tubes and at the end of every day, every week and every month you shrug your shoulders and say, "Nope, we still ain't found a cure."

But you still get paid.

That's one tough gig!

Win or lose you take home a fancy salary; and get to comp those expensive lunches with your other scientists.

My wife pays for that.

Let me tell you something about global warming.

We're enjoying unseasonably fine weather. So what if a bit of the North Pole drops off?

Sounds like a pretty good bargain to me.

Besides, in a few thousand years the likelihood is we'll be dead so who really gives a crap if the world has fried by then?

Anyway, we'll be living in apartment blocks on Pluto.

Luckily I sat my little girl down and articulated this to her and now she's stopped her babbling.

I think you ought to quit your scaremongering tactics and stop frightening the wits out of little girls like my Roxanne.

Raymond Delauney

Previous | Next | Back to Messages

| Delete | Reply ⌄ | Forward ⌄ | Spam | Move.. ⌄ |

Date:	Wed, 01 Nov 2006 11:58:01 -0600
From:	"Gerry Zennon" <gerryzennon@savethegreenball.net>
To:	"raymond delauney" <raymonddelauney@yahoo.co.uk>
Subject:	Re: Global warming

Dear Raymond,

I am sorry that the truth and your daughter's ecological sense makes you so angry. I have spent my entire life studying ecology, 28 years of school. And yes, I do think I am smarter (at least regarding climate change) than you. You are doing a grave disservice to your daughter by failing to educate yourself.

Warm regards,

Dr. Gerry Zennon

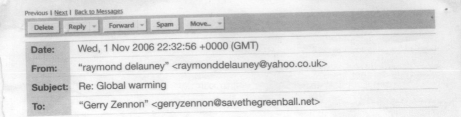

Delete   Reply ▾   Forward ▾   Spam   Move... ▾

Date:	Wed, 1 Nov 2006 22:32:56 +0000 (GMT)
From:	"raymond delauney" <raymonddelauney@yahoo.co.uk>
Subject:	Re: Global warming
To:	"Gerry Zennon" <gerryzennon@savethegreenball.net>

Gerry,

You know what I've just spent the last 4 minutes doing?

Leaning out of my bedroom window emptying a WHOLE can of deodorant into the sky. I probably wouldn't have done that had you not insulted me by claiming to be smarter than me. Before you insult someone you should really have a think about the consequences of your actions.

Let me tell you something, buddy. You think you're smarter than me by spending 28 years at school? I was asked to leave when I was 15. When you were still in school I was out earning for an extra 13 years.

Last year I banked £50,000. That's right, 50 big ones. I doubt you get that much learning economy for 28 years. So who do you think is smarter now?

I did my schooling at the University of Hard Knocks – in Chichester.

My dad used to beat me regularly and I hated him for it. I remember kids saying to me, "My dad can beat up your dad." I'd get excited and say: "Really? When can he come round and do it?"

But you know something? If I learnt anything from him it was to stand up for yourself. If someone is being rude to you then you shouldn't accept it. You should whack them in the face, hard.

People like you think we should give up flying aeroplanes and driving motor cars?

Don't think so buddy. This planet, like life itself, has an expiry date.

While we're here we might as well party.

I will accept an apology if you are prepared to issue one.

Raymond

Date:	Wed, 01 Nov 2006 17:05:08 -0600
From:	"Gerry Zennon" <gerryzennon@savethegreenball.net>
To:	"raymond delauney" <raymonddelauney@yahoo.co.uk>
Subject:	Re: Global warming

Go fuck yourself and then get some help.

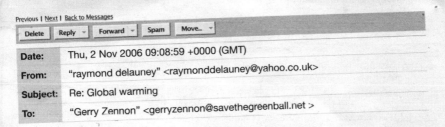

Date:	Thu, 2 Nov 2006 09:08:59 +0000 (GMT)
From:	"raymond delauney" <raymonddelauney@yahoo.co.uk>
Subject:	Re: Global warming
To:	"Gerry Zennon" <gerryzennon@savethegreenball.net >

Gerry,

You know what I've just done? Left the engine running on my car with the garage door left open.

I don't have unleaded.

If you use foul and abusive language on me again I swear I will find a small tree somewhere, anywhere, and chop it down.

Great isn't it. An extra 28 years at school and you resort to playground talk as soon as you start losing an argument. I think I've proved a point.

Regards,

Raymond Delauney

NO REPLY

MISSING LEG

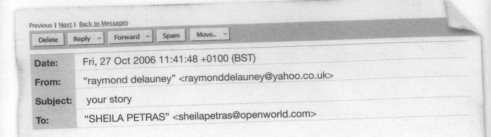

Delete   Reply ▾   Forward ▾   Spam   Move... ▾

Date:	Fri, 27 Oct 2006 11:41:48 +0100 (BST)
From:	"raymond delauney" <raymonddelauney@yahoo.co.uk>
Subject:	your story
To:	"SHEILA PETRAS" <sheilapetras@openworld.com>

I have a story that I want to sell to your magazine.

I had an operation to have a gangrenous leg amputated and after the op the doctor told me there was good news and bad news. The bad news was they'd amputated the wrong leg. The good news was they thought they might be able to save the other one.

How much do you think this story is worth?

Delete   Reply ▾   Forward ▾   Spam   Move... ▾

Date:	Fri, 27 Oct 2006 11:49:34 +0100 (BST)
From:	"SHEILA PETRAS" <sheilapetras@openworld.com>
Subject:	Re: your story
To:	raymonddelauney@yahoo.co.uk

Thank you for your email Raymond, can you email me your phone number over please?

Kind Regards
Sheila Petras

sheilapetras@openworld.com

Date:	Fri, 27 Oct 2006 11:55:48 +0100 (BST)
From:	"raymond delauney" <raymonddelauney@yahoo.co.uk>
Subject:	Re: your story
To:	"SHEILA PETRAS" <sheilapetras@openworld.com>

Hi Sheila,

My mobile phone is downstairs at the moment and my helper won't be in until around 4 o'clock. She's from South Africa and is a bloody rotten timekeeper.

She talks non-stop about her travels and the danger of living in South Africa – like I'm interested.

I could get the phone myself but a Kentucky fried chicken bag is obstructing the stannah stair lift and frankly I can't be bothered to make the effort to remove it.

I am in front of a computer though.

Could you tell me how much this story is worth – if anything. I'm not prepared to sell it and have people sympathise/pity me unless I receive some financial stimulus. I can provide before/after pics.

Regards,

Raymond

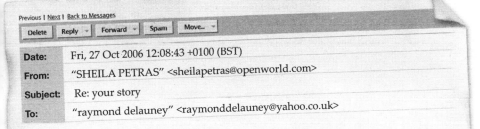

Date:	Fri, 27 Oct 2006 12:08:43 +0100 (BST)
From:	"SHEILA PETRAS" <sheilapetras@openworld.com>
Subject:	Re: your story
To:	"raymond delauney" <raymonddelauney@yahoo.co.uk>

Hi Raymond,

Before I can give you a price for your story I need to ask you a few questions. First of all: When did this happen, which hospital was it and I need to know how much the offer was that you turned down?

Look forward to hearing from you.

Sheila

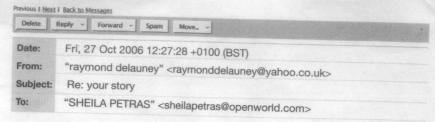

Date:	Fri, 27 Oct 2006 12:27:28 +0100 (BST)
From:	"raymond delauney" <raymonddelauney@yahoo.co.uk>
Subject:	Re: your story
To:	"SHEILA PETRAS" <sheilapetras@openworld.com>

Hello Sheila,

It might have been polite to start your mail with something along the lines of, "I'm terribly sorry to hear about this tragic tale etc."

I guess you journalists are just interested in stories. That's okay, it doesn't bother me.

My only concern is that publication of the story may jeopardise my court case in some way. I'm not sure I can reveal the name of the surgeon (he's blaming the nurse and she's saying she acted under orders).

We could report the facts – which cannot be disputed.

I have a personal aspect to the story some might find amusing although at the time it really enraged me.

Can you give me a ballpark figure at least? I'm not selling for peanuts so it may make sense to let me know the sum before we proceed any further.
Obviously I am aware if I gave you the hospital you could probably get the story yourself for free.

I'll be brutally honest. Like you, I'm after sole gain. I'm not at all interested in the welfare of your career nor am I particularly thrilled at the prospect of briefly titillating or horrifying your readership. I merely want to secure myself as much money as I can.

Raymond

Date:	Fri, 27 Oct 2006 12:38:48 +0100 (BST)
From:	"SHEILA PETRAS" <sheilapetras@openworld.com>
Subject:	Re: your story
To:	"raymond delauney" <raymonddelauney@yahoo.co.uk>

Hi Raymond,

Without a doubt it is terrible what happened to you, and US journalists are not just in it just for sole gain! We have a duty to report the facts of any story to the general public. Stories such as yours are not titillated or horrified for our readership. I can assure you we would take your story very seriously indeed.

Meanwhile, I can't give you a fair ball park figure until I have the details I need to put before a publication. I doubt it very much that the hospital would give us the story as it's not something that they would want out in the public domain. I am not interested in obtaining any story for free! Our job here is to get YOU the best deal possible.

If you wish to answer my questions I am in a position to help you, however, if you decided not to then I will take this opportunity to wish you all the best.

Kind regards

Sheila

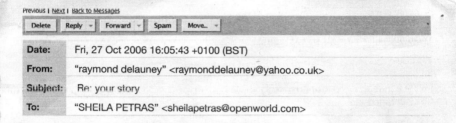

Delete	Reply ▾	Forward ▾	Spam	Move... ▾	

Date:	Fri, 27 Oct 2006 16:05:43 +0100 (BST)
From:	"raymond delauney" <raymonddelauney@yahoo.co.uk>
Subject:	Re: your story
To:	"SHEILA PETRAS" <sheilapetras@openworld.com>

Sheila,

I need to get to the bottom of things here. Do you work for Take A Break magazine? Are you a journalist yourself? I take it an affirmative answer to both of those questions is incompatible.

By the way, I find it intensely annoying when people capitalise for emphasis. I might be minus a leg but as far as I'm aware my eyesight is fine, i.e. "US journalists are not just in it for sole gain."

Anyway, that reads as if American journalists are not in things for their own gain. And they are, with the gain usually being in weight department.

Let's get down to brass tacks:

You are being deliberately miserly with any forthcoming information regarding fees, in the same way, I suspect, that there are no price tags attached to clothes in those expensive clothes shops I can't afford to shop in.

I'm guessing I ain't got a lot to offer, have you? I've turned down £350,000 compensation so far. That might sound an awfully large sum but would you swap YOUR leg for it?

Now, Sheila, how much can you get ME?

Raymond

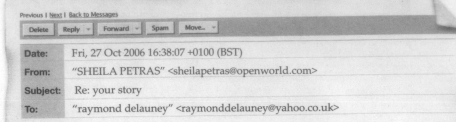

Delete | Reply ▾ | Forward ▾ | Spam | Move... ▾

Date:	Fri, 27 Oct 2006 16:38:07 +0100 (BST)
From:	"SHEILA PETRAS" <sheilapetras@openworld.com>
Subject:	Re: your story
To:	"raymond delauney" <raymonddelauney@yahoo.co.uk>

Dear Raymond,

I am not employed by Take A Break. We are agents for all of the UK magazines and National newspapers. Our/my job is to represent you within the national media. I have spoken to my colleagues on the national newspapers and the general figure that I am getting back is around £5,000 for your story.

Regards

Sheila

Delete | Reply ▾ | Forward ▾ | Spam | Move... ▾

Date:	Wed, 7 Mar 2007 17:45:27 +0000 (GMT)
From:	"raymond delauney" <raymonddelauney@yahoo.co.uk>
Subject:	Re: My Dilemma
To:	"SHEILA PETRAS" <sheilapetras@openworld.com>

Sheila,

Thanks for (eventually) getting back to me with a figure, the size of which disappoints.

I would be prepared to do business for £10,000. I need to know how much your cut of the cake will be. If it's 10 per cent I think that's way too much.

I mean, all you're doing is making a phone call for £1,000 whereas my commitment to the story is 50% of my total leg count.

I am fearful of people seeing the article in the press and of being the subject of feigned pity, which is all I seem to get these days. Mind, you didn't even bother to feign it.

Like most things in life there is a price for doing things you don't want to do and for me it's £10k. It'll tide me over until the fat cheque arrives.

I feel my story would be worth the extra cash for the reasons I have listed below:

Being dumped by my girlfriend just three months later – for a recruitment consultant.

Not being given a replacement remote control for the TV in my hospital room after throwing the original out of the hospital window.

I was amazingly berated by hospital staff for being (three astonishing quotes)

"Continually feeling sorry for himself and being uncompromisingly stubborn and difficult"

"Easily the most sarcastic attitude person I've ever met"

"Naturally rude"

Even worse than being insulted by lowly hospital staff was being patronised during a counselling session. One hippie counsellor informed me I "would still be able to do most of the things I did before the accident".

Really? What about the triple jump? To succeed in the event you have to run the 100 metres in approx 12 seconds and as far as I know it's almost impossible to reach that speed by hopping. Besides, the event is known as the hop, skip and jump. For me it would be one continuous hop.

I really felt like hitting him after he said that and would have done had he been within arm's reach. Get back to me with a reply as soon as you can.

Raymond

Delete	Reply ⌄	Forward ⌄	Spam	Move... ⌄

Date: Mon, 30 Oct 2006 10:08:09 +0000 (GMT)

From: "raymond delauney" <raymonddelauney@yahoo.co.uk>

Subject: Re: your story

To: "SHEILA PETRAS" <sheilapetras@openworld.com>

Dear Raymond,

Sorry I was not able to get back to you sooner but we are very busy here as we handle in excess of 30 features a day as well as it being the weekend.

As it states on my website, our service to you is entirely free of charge nor do we take any commission. I will check with the newspapers if they are prepared to go up to 10k for your story, however, I doubt it. As it stands at the moment I have no proof of your story. So if it is possible, could you please email me some form of confirmation that what you are saying is in fact the case?

With regards to payment for your story, it is not the publication's obligation to compensate you for the hospital remote control or the fact your girlfriend dumped you and this will not be reflected in any monies offered to you for your story. You will be offered payment for your story on its merits alone.

Regards

Sheila Petras

| Delete | Reply ▾ | Forward ▾ | Spam | Move... ▾ |

Date:	Mon, 30 Oct 2006 17:16:00 +0000 (GMT)
From:	"raymond delauney" <raymonddelauney@yahoo.co.uk>
Subject:	Re: your story
To:	"SHEILA PETRAS" <sheilapetras@openworld.com>

Sheila,

You are really testing my patience. I understand in your job, which as far as I can see is basically a 'middleman', the advantages of being abrasive. But treating me like the village idiot is hardly likely to expedite matters.

You claim you don't charge commission. Poppycock. You take a fee off the newspaper. This money would normally go to the guy who sells the story (in this case me). So yes, indirectly you are charging a fee. Effectively taking money from my pocket under the pretext of doing me a favour.

I mentioned being dumped by the girlfriend (the bitch) not because I'm after sympathy but because it adds an extra dimension to the human-interest angle of the story.

And another thing I find insulting. Why do you keep badgering me for proof? What do you suggest I do – turn up at your office carrying a severed leg under my arm just to satisfy your perverse curiosity?

Or do you think a one-legged man is pulling your leg?

I'll be frank here, Sheila. I've lost any semblance of confidence I ever had in you.

I need you to forward me the contact details of the newspapers you think might be interested in the story and I'll see if I can negotiate a deal myself. If successful I'll recommend you to friends, though I don't have many now.

List names and numbers in order of who is most likely to buy.

Raymond

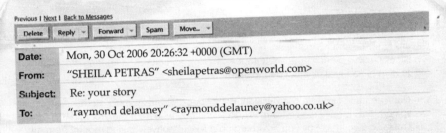

Previous | Next | Back to Messages

| Delete | Reply ▾ | Forward ▾ | Spam | Move... ▾ |

Date:	Mon, 30 Oct 2006 20:26:32 +0000 (GMT)
From:	"SHEILA PETRAS" <sheilapetras@openworld.com>
Subject:	Re: your story
To:	"raymond delauney" <raymonddelauney@yahoo.co.uk>

Raymond,

I am very busy with people who really want to tell their stories. I do not have time for your rudeness and arrogance.

Please do not contact me again.

Sheila Petras

END OF CORRESPONDENCE

ARCHIVE FOOTAGE

What were you doing in the 1970s?

Did you record it at all on your film camera?

Family holidays, parties, events of the decade, the strikes, the 3-day week etc. Do you still have the footage?

How would you like to share it with the world?

A top TV company are making a series about the 70s and are looking for footage of real people and their families who lived through the decade and have their own footage to prove it (8mm, 16mm, 9.5mm). You should also be happy to appear on screen to talk about life then, illustrated by your own unique footage.

So if you think you've got some great films to show just what life was like then and want to share it please call...

Previous | Next | Back to Messages

Delete | Reply ▾ | Forward ▾ | Spam | Move... ▾

Date:	Tue, 8 Nov 2005 10:22:50 +0000 (GMT)
From:	"raymond delauney" <raymonddelauney@yahoo.co.uk>
Subject:	1970s
To:	lucy.puddle@archivetv.biz

Hello,

A friend of mine, Paul Tadd, saw your request for video footage of events that took place in the 1970s and immediately contacted me.

I was born in the late 1960s and as I recall my father was one of the earliest owners of a super 8 video camera. He was seldom without it during any event of note throughout the 70s, right up until the day he died, in a boating accident in Tilbury, 1986.

Unfortunately father's main hobby was bird watching, consequently we have endless footage of rustling trees and not much else.

However he did take the camera out on special events and he recorded the 1977 Silver Jubilee celebrations in Stratford, east London.

The day was quite memorable because people we didn't really socialise with were exceptionally jolly toward us and I remember it being the best street party ever. Oddly, despite such unprecedented friendliness the good spirits evaporated the next day and everyone reverted back to acting like strangers, almost as if the incident never took place.

In the film everyone looks typically passé in long hair, big collars and huge flares. The day turned a bit sour when, out of the blue, a huge, demented woman, with a face like a careless beekeeper, brutally attacked another lady. The two women rolled around on the floor tugging forcibly at each other's hair. A table of cheese and pineapple sticks is knocked over during the struggle as people made room for the contest to continue. All the onlookers did was look on.

The victim of the assault was Mrs Froud, who lived three doors away from us, she worked in the chip shop three days a week and would always give us an extra large portion of chips or throw in the odd pickled onion for free when me or my brothers came in. She was quite kind to us. Her legs seemed fatter than the rest of her body and quite often one leg or both sported an unsightly bruise the cause of which was never apparent.

I had never seen the big woman assailant before – and I never saw her since. She fought like her life depended on it and gave poor Mrs Froud a terrible beating. You didn't step in the way of two women fighting in east London in those days because if you did someone was sure to step in and batter you for no good reason. That's just the way things work.

Nobody stopped the two women fighting and father kept filming until Mrs Froud smashed a jubilee mug over the crazy woman's head. This dazed her for long enough to make her release her grip on Mrs Froud, who took her chance to scurry off, her head is seen bleeding quite badly with cheese and pineapple matted in her hair.

Is any of this worth money?

Best regards,

Raymond Delauney

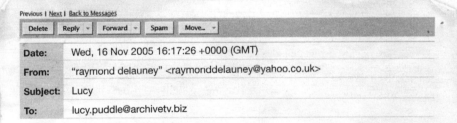

| Delete | Reply ⌄ | Forward ⌄ | Spam | Move... ⌄ |

Date:	Wed, 16 Nov 2005 16:17:26 +0000 (GMT)
From:	"raymond delauney" <raymonddelauney@yahoo.co.uk>
Subject:	Lucy
To:	lucy.puddle@archivetv.biz

Lucy,

I sent you a mail in response to your plea for video footage of the seventies and you haven't even bothered to reply.

Who do you think you are? Some big shot producer?

Get back in touch with me and we'll talk money – I think I have something you might be interested in.

Don't drag your heels, honey.

Raymond Delauney

Delete | Reply ▾ | Forward ▾ | Spam | Move... ▾

Subject:	RE: Lucy
Date:	Thu, 17 Nov 2005 17:14:11 -0000
From:	"Lucy Puddle" <lucy.puddle@archivetv.biz>
To:	"raymond delauney" <raymonddelauney@yahoo.co.uk>

Dear Raymond,

Firstly I must apologise for not responding to your email, I thought I had but obviously not, so sorry and no I am not some big shot producer just a lowly overworked researcher.

Your footage of the jubilee sounds excellent and your email was beautifully written and very funny, a perfect antidote to all the happy smiling faces type stuff – however my producer's concern was about clearing it for TV are you still in touch with Mrs Froud or the crazy woman – would it be possible to get in touch with them at all?

I am talking to my producer next week about what stuff we are going to call in – your stuff isn't exactly on brief but does sound great – is it in colour? How long does the jubliee film last for is it still in super 8 format?

Best Regards

Lucy Puddle – Researcher

Delete | Reply ▾ | Forward ▾ | Spam | Move... ▾

Date:	Sun, 20 Nov 2005 17:39:41 +0000 (GMT)
From:	"raymond delauney" <raymonddelauney@yahoo.co.uk>
Subject:	RE: Lucy
To:	"Lucy Puddle" <lucy.puddle@archivetv.biz>

Hi Lucy,

If I'd known I was communicating with a 'lowly researcher' the tone I adopted in my last mail wouldn't have been so uncharacteristically hostile.

Astonishingly, for a man of my aptitude and ability, I'm a low man on the totem pole too and, worse still, ensnared in a ghastly, loveless marriage.

Okay, let's get down to brass tacks.

The film is in super 8, colour and lasts approximately 12 minutes. The brutally explicit fight scene involving Mrs Froud and the crazy woman extends to precisely 18 seconds of film.

I feel that your 'Seventies Show' (lousy title, incidentally) would benefit enormously with

this calibre of footage. I would propose using my piece as a teaser intro.
First we show some tame clip of, say Keith Chegwin prancing about in one of his technicoloured jumpers, thus lowering viewers' expectations, before a voiceover solemnly declares, "… but it wasn't all fun and frolics In the Seventies". Cut to Mrs Froud shattering the Jubilee mug over the crazy woman's melon, rendering the hideous beast stunned and senseless.

These violent images could be offset slightly by the comedic value of two women rolling around on the deck like a couple of out of condition wrestlers, their unkempt hair entangled with pineapple and cheese swizzles. The apathetic look of a boy in the background, wearing a tightly sprung perm, is enlightening, as he is clearly more interested in stealing and scoffing the spilt cake than the bitch fight taking place before him. Cruelty was commonplace in the east end during the Seventies.

I think I can get in touch with Froud. One of my brothers enjoyed a 12-hour relationship with her daughter a few years ago. The girl, if memory serves, is a pasty-faced individual of low intellect who has had the misfortune to inherit her mother's plump pins. The crazy woman, possibly by virtue of being crazy, is virtually impossible to trace. I wouldn't be at all surprised if she's snuffed it.

Is the programme going to be on ITV? I do hope so as that is where the dough is.

What will the syndication rights be if the clip is shown worldwide? If you get me a good deal, Lucy, I'll cut you in on 10%.

I'll try and arrange a meeting with Froud.

I need to catch a break.

Best regards,

Raymond Delauney

Delete	Reply ▾	Forward ▾	Spam	Move... ▾	

Subject:	RE: Lucy
Date:	Tue, 22 Nov 2005 12:37:55 -0000
From:	"Lucy Puddle" <lucy.puddle@archivetv.biz>
To:	"raymond delauney" <raymonddelauney@yahoo.co.uk>

OK Raymond – let's calm down here, the programme is for channel 5 so we are hardly awash with cash, more like wringing out our tea bags and reusing them, if you see what I mean – however if we do use your footage there may be some nominal sum and also we can convert it to DVD for you – we have to do that to view it.

If you think you can get hold of Mrs Froud and she will agree to it being shown, what I suggest is that we call it in – I can send a courier for it to make sure that it is safe and then I can get my producers to have a look... let me know what you think. Your email has just arrived as I was finishing this one.

Thanks

Lucy

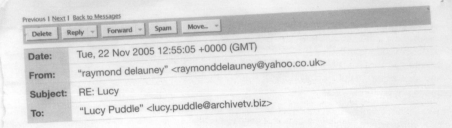

Date:	Tue, 22 Nov 2005 12:55:05 +0000 (GMT)
From:	"raymond delauney" <raymonddelauney@yahoo.co.uk>
Subject:	RE: Lucy
To:	"Lucy Puddle" <lucy.puddle@archivetv.biz>

Lucy,

I'm meeting with Froud tonight. Got her number from her daughter. She didn't want to know at first but I promised her £20 and her attitude changed completely. She now lives in Kent.

Try not to use vulgar words like 'nominal fee'. Frankly, that frightened me. Don't forget I'm going to cut you in on this one so maybe we should think about inflating the fee. More cake for all parties concerned.

Remember, if this series goes well it could be Earl Grey all round (bags used once).

I'll get back to you, tomorrow.

Incidentally, are you good looking?

Regards,

Raymond

Subject:	sorry
Date:	Wed, 23 Nov 2005 12:23:06 -0000
From:	"Lucy Puddle" <lucy.puddle@archivetv.biz>
To:	"raymond delauney" <raymonddelauney@yahoo.co.uk>

I just thought I'd let you know before you do any more work that in a meeting this morning my producer has declared that your footage will not fit in with his film, so thanks but no thanks.

Best Regards

Lucy

Lucy Puddle – Researcher

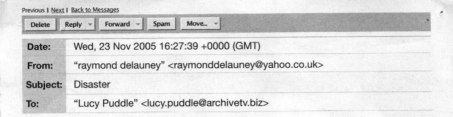

Date:	Wed, 23 Nov 2005 16:27:39 +0000 (GMT)
From:	"raymond delauney" <raymonddelauney@yahoo.co.uk>
Subject:	Disaster
To:	"Lucy Puddle" <lucy.puddle@archivetv.biz>

Lucy,

I got it wrong, badly wrong.

The crazy woman isn't the crazy woman. Mrs Froud Is the crazy woman.

I drove over to Tunbridge Wells last night armed with projector and tape with the intention of attaining Froud's permission to use the film. As it turned out, unbeknownst to me, I needn't have bothered.

I tracked down the address Froud had given me over the phone to a grungy terrace in the dimly lit backwaters of Kent. I approached her house with justified trepidation. The entire front face of the house was covered in graffiti, daubed in red paint on the front door was the ominous message 'Not Wanted'. The lawn was wildly overgrown and littered with various car parts, none of which looked functional.

I was shocked to see Froud answer the front door. She had gained a conspicuous amount of weight since I last saw her; the size of her body had caught up and surpassed the balloon like quality of her legs. They almost looked scrawny in comparison now, except for two dreadfully swollen ankles. Her hair had turned completely grey.

She immediately asked for the £20 I had promised her on the phone and only once I'd handed it over did she stand to one side and allow me access to her threadbare dwelling. As she did so I became nervously aware of an elderly man in a dressing gown standing a few steps behind her. Either the hall or the man smelt strongly of damp.

All my attempts at conversation led down one-word cul de sac responses. I asked her how her husband was, a slip-up I regretted as soon as the words had spilled from my mouth.

"Dead," she replied without a trace of sentiment.

I muddled on, enquiring as to whether she saw much of her daughter.

"No."

I attempted to lighten the mood by revealing something of my past. I spoke with what I hoped was a disarming smile. I revealed I was in the process of getting a divorce (true) and that my wife and I had agreed on a fifty-fifty split. Fifty per cent to the wife and fifty per cent to her lawyer. This revelation failed to garner any morsel of sympathy or interest and the old man by this point appeared to be satisfying an itch inside the lower regions of his gown.

I decided to set up the projector and tape in silence, thus minimising the amount of time I was forced to spend in their company. Up to this point I had been unspecific as to the exact content of the tape. By way of introduction I announced the film I was about to show "represented a snatch of the Seventies".

As the tape whirled into life I stood a cautionary step behind Froud so as to keep a beady eye on her. As the fight scene approached I monitored the old woman's gaze as she scrutinised every scene played out before her. It was as if she had been magically transported back into the past.

As the money scene approached I thought it prudent to forewarn her that the forthcoming episode may prove disturbing. "A little fracas between two ladies takes place soon," I nervously intoned, but by this time I think she knew what was coming.

Her reaction was not exactly what I had anticipated. She bellowed furiously, then lunged, first toward me, then the projector. She ripped the tape from the machine and commenced to shred it with all the force she could muster, which was quite a lot.

The old man began to snarl menacingly, edging nearer to me as he did so. At this point I heard scuffled sounds somewhere above me as if people disturbed by the noise below began mobilising themselves.

Worried that further freaks might soon descend and set upon me, I snatched my projector and fled the hovel as fast as I possibly could.

I returned home shaken, £20 lighter and minus my father's tape.

Then, I receive a terse mail from you saying that I needn't have bothered, as you wouldn't have used it anyway

I think this is a pretty shabby way to treat someone.

Disappointed,

Raymond Delauney

Delete **Reply** ▾ **Forward** ▾ **Spam** **Move...** ▾

Subject:	RE: Disaster
Date:	Wed, 23 Nov 2005 18:05:09 -0000
From:	"Lucy Puddle" <lucy.puddle@archivetv.biz>
To:	"raymond delauney" <raymonddelauney@yahoo.co.uk>

Raymond,

Big apologies for all your time and effort but the whims of producers are notoriously fickle. Sometimes their minds are as easy to read as tea leaves. Such a sad and sorry story but from my point of view quite a lucky one.

Thank goodness my producer hadn't set his heart on the footage only to find that it had been shredded by the terrifying Froud – had that been the case!

I feel sure that he would have sent me round to Tunbridge Wells myself to request that she stick it back together with sellotape – which after your chilling tale is not a mission that I would have relished.

Good luck with your divorce I do so hope you had managed to offshore most of your assets.

Best Regards

Lucy

END OF CORRESPONDENCE

MEDIA SALES

On behalf of our famous client, we are looking for dynamic candidates with in excess of one year's media sales experience. Knowledge of online environments would be an advantage, but not essential. Since your role will be selling advertising and sponsorship for the biggest name in cricket you will be passionate about the sport as well as self-motivated, a great presenter and negotiator who would relish the opportunity to take a step up and work on a big name online brand. You will be responsible for ten core clients as well as winning new business and seeking out new promotional opportunities. If you have the above experience then please forward your CV to the email address below:

Previous | Next | Back to Messages

| Delete | Reply ▾ | Forward ▾ | Spam | Move... ▾ |

Date:	Tue, 21 Nov 2005 12:48:23 +0000 (GMT)
From:	"raymond delauney" <raymonddelauney@yahoo.co.uk>
Subject:	Cricket Job
To:	matt@onthegreentalent.com

Hi Matt,

I think I should have the cricket job currently advertised in the Guardian.

I have no sales experience whatsoever but my knowledge on cricket is unsurpassed. Did you know, for example, that Len Hutton is the only cricketer who has ever been given out obstructing the field? That is 100% true. I have more gems where that came from.

I think I can develop the sales aspect of the job in time as I am a very persuasive talker.

Would the position involve visiting cricket grounds and watching matches?

Best regards,

Raymond Delauney

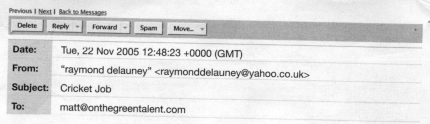

Date: Tue, 22 Nov 2005 12:48:23 +0000 (GMT)

From: "raymond delauney" <raymonddelauney@yahoo.co.uk>

Subject: Cricket Job

To: matt@onthegreentalent.com

Hi Matt,

Further to my mail yesterday.

I would like to emphasise the interest shown in the position and can confirm I am ready and able to start as and when required.

I neglected to mention in my earlier mail that I have some limited sales experience working in a shoe shop one summer. It's a base to work from I guess. I suppose you could say I've looked good in the nets and am anxious to open the batting!

P.S.

Wilfred Rhodes (England) batted in all eleven positions in Test cricket.

His feat was emulated by Vinoo Mankad.

Hopefully,

Raymond Delauney

From: "Matt Hawkins" <matt@onthegreentalent.com>

To: "'raymond delauney'" <raymonddelauney@yahoo.co.uk>

Subject: CV?

Date: Tue, 22 Nov 2005 13:03:16 -0000

Hi Raymond,

Thanks for your email.

If you would like to apply for the vacancy please forward your CV as requested.

Thanks,

Matt

Delete | Reply ▾ | Forward ▾ | Spam | Move... ▾

Date:	Tue, 22 Nov 2005 14:23:09 +0000 (GMT)
From:	"raymond delauney" <raymonddelauney@yahoo.co.uk>
Subject:	Re: CV?
To:	"Matt Hawkins" <matt@onthegreentalent.com>

Matt,

What CV?

I left school this summer and haven't done anything yet.

What's the point of sending in a blank CV?

What are you? A talent spotter as you claim to be or some who merely sits on their arse scanning CVs?

C'mon Matt, use your melon and grant me an interview slot. I'll do the rest from there.

Nobody knows more about the game of cricket than me.

I always close out my mails with an interesting piece of cricket trivia.

Marvan Attapatu (Sri Lanka) had scores of 0,0,1,0,0,0 in his first three Test matches. No prizes for guessing what he scored in his first one-dayer. Yes – 0!

Please get back to me with an interview date.

Regards,

Raymond

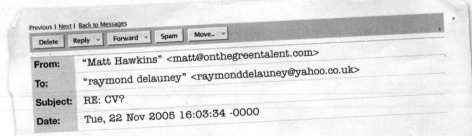

Delete | Reply ▾ | Forward ▾ | Spam | Move... ▾

From:	"Matt Hawkins" <matt@onthegreentalent.com>
To:	"raymond delauney" <raymonddelauney@yahoo.co.uk>
Subject:	RE: CV?
Date:	Tue, 22 Nov 2005 16:03:34 -0000

Dear Raymond,

Wow – if you've done nothing since summer you must be bored. But then I'd guessed that you were.

It's rare that I can tell a candidate that they've failed even before I've met them or seen their CV. However, in this case I'm prepared to make an exception.

So – thank you for your interest, we're sorry but we won't be pursuing your application any further.

Best,

Matt

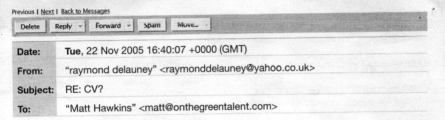

| Delete | Reply ▾ | Forward ▾ | Spam | Move... |

Date:	**Tue**, 22 Nov 2005 16:40:07 +0000 (GMT)
From:	"raymond delauney" <raymonddelauney@yahoo.co.uk>
Subject:	RE: CV?
To:	"Matt Hawkins" <matt@onthegreentalent.com>

Matt,

I didn't care for the attitude in your last mail.

Experience has told me that the most effective response to an insult is silence.

However in this case I felt I couldn't turn down the opportunity of verbally abusing a mere recruitment consultant with delusions of grandeur. Perhaps you'll graduate to telesales in the years ahead?

I'll keep this simple, unoriginal and uncomplicated.

You smarmy twit.

I intend to find out who precisely is advertising this job, apply to them directly, secure the position and cut you out of any commission.

Nobody knows more about the game of cricket than me.

Sir Donald Bradman retired from Test cricket having scored 6,996 runs at an average of 99.94. In his last Test innings he needed 4 runs to have an average of 100. He scored 0!

Raymond Delauney

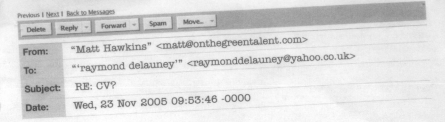

Previous | Next | Back to Messages

Delete | Reply ⌄ | Forward ⌄ | Spam | Move... ⌄

From:	"Matt Hawkins" <matt@onthegreentalent.com>
To:	"'raymond delauney'" <raymonddelauney@yahoo.co.uk>
Subject:	RE: CV?
Date:	Wed, 23 Nov 2005 09:53:46 -0000

Dear Ray,

(I feel I can call you Ray now.)

At OnTheGreen we have the highest standards of candidate screening procedure – to eliminate timewasters, I'm sure you understand.

However, your persistence, demonstrable love of the sport and beautifully crafted arguments have paid off. You may be just the fellow we're seeking for this position.

When are you free for interview?

Best,

Matt

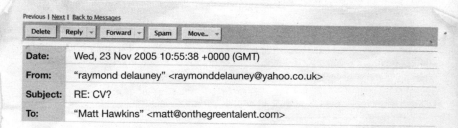

Previous | Next | Back to Messages

Delete | Reply ⌄ | Forward ⌄ | Spam | Move... ⌄

Date:	Wed, 23 Nov 2005 10:55:38 +0000 (GMT)
From:	"raymond delauney" <raymonddelauney@yahoo.co.uk>
Subject:	RE: CV?
To:	"Matt Hawkins" <matt@onthegreentalent.com>

Matt,

Yippee!

All credit to you for attempting to bury the hatchet.

Apologies for losing my temper earlier, which was due in main to your contemptible rudeness. I'm willing to forgive and forget and move on.

In the circumstances I believe this course of action would be best for all parties concerned – you, me and the firm anxious to employ me.

It's a win/win/win as you sales people might say! I'll be taking up paid work, they'll be bolstering their ranks with a cricket genius and you'll be skimming off my wages. I don't mind this as I could do with catching a break here.

In case you are wondering I also play the game to a decent standard and can achieve reverse swing with the old ball. Do they have a cricket team?

Let's get down to brass tacks:

Where and when is my interview?

Get back to me at your earliest convenience.

Trivia: Never have the first four batsman of a team each scored centuries in the same Test innings. However, playing England at Lord's in June, 1993 Australia's scorecard looked like this:

Mark Taylor	111
Michael Slater	152
David Boon	164
Mark Waugh	99

Regards,

Raymond Delauney

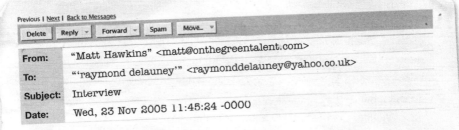

Delete   Reply ▾   Forward ▾   Spam   Move... ▾

From:	"Matt Hawkins" <matt@onthegreentalent.com>
To:	"'raymond delauney'" <raymonddelauney@yahoo.co.uk>
Subject:	Interview
Date:	Wed, 23 Nov 2005 11:45:24 -0000

Hi Ray,

Thanks for your flexibility. I'm free for interview on Friday this week – how about a lunchtime slot?

Please be aware that candidates are required to turn up for interview in full cricketing flannels, protective pads and jockstrap.

(This applies to all OnTheGreen media sales positions.)

Best,

Matt

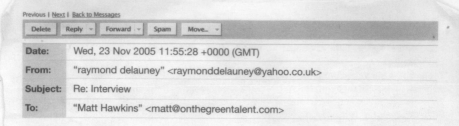

Delete Reply ▼ Forward ▼ Spam Move... ▼

Date:	Wed, 23 Nov 2005 11:55:28 +0000 (GMT)
From:	"raymond delauney" <raymonddelauney@yahoo.co.uk>
Subject:	Re: Interview
To:	"Matt Hawkins" <matt@onthegreentalent.com>

Hawkins,

I think I'll just bring the bat.
Stop wasting my time, you oaf.

Raymond

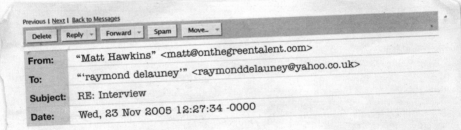

Delete Reply ▼ Forward ▼ Spam Move... ▼

From:	"Matt Hawkins" <matt@onthegreentalent.com>
To:	"'raymond delauney'" <raymonddelauney@yahoo.co.uk>
Subject:	RE: Interview
Date:	Wed, 23 Nov 2005 12:27:34 -0000

Oh dear.

Lost the usual attitude?

And no trivia!

Words have failed you once again Raymond. Or – in a final cricketing metaphor, you appear to have been stumped.

And on that note, it's time to call a halt to play, draw the covers over and send you home. Sadly, this correspondence is over.

It's been a pleasure.

Matt

| Delete | Reply ▾ | Forward ▾ | Spam | Move.. ▾ |

Date:	Wed, 23 Nov 2005 12:55:58 +0000 (GMT)
From:	"raymond delauney" <raymonddelauney@yahoo.co.uk>
Subject:	RE: Interview
To:	"Matt Hawkins" <matt@onthegreentalent.com>

Hawkins,

I think the last innings has yet to be played and it is I who will make the final declaration.

As the old saying goes, "those that can do and those that have no fucking discernible talent whatsoever work as recruitment consultants."

Raymond Delauney

END OF CORRESPONDENCE

DRUG TRIALS

Have you ever experimented with illicit drugs?

This includes Cocaine, Amphetamines, Cannabis and LSD.

If so and you are a healthy male aged between 25–50, who speaks English as a first language, then you may be eligible to take part in our medical research at Thorpe Hospital.

We are now in the closing stages of our research and we are particularly keen to find males who have experimented with cocaine and/or amphetamines, but who have NEVER used Ecstasy. Hair and urine analysis will be conducted on all participants to verify the accuracy of reported drug use.

The study involves 2 brain scans and some psychological tests over 1 working day.

Participants will be reimbursed £70 for their time plus expenses and receive a picture of their brain.

If you are interested, please email a contact telephone number and the best time to call to you to leslie.bradshaw@crl.mro.ac.uk

Your participation is totally confidential.

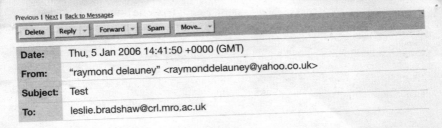

Previous I Next I Back to Messages

Delete | Reply ▾ | Forward ▾ | Spam | Move... ▾

Date:	Thu, 5 Jan 2006 14:41:50 +0000 (GMT)
From:	"raymond delauney" <raymonddelauney@yahoo.co.uk>
Subject:	Test
To:	leslie.bradshaw@crl.mro.ac.uk

Hi Leslie,

I think I'm the type of guinea pig you're looking for.

I've tried out most drugs available. I must stress I am not addicted to anything. I ply myself socially and only with what I feel agrees with my body and its needs.

I like a line or two of Charlie – who doesn't?

Apart from the snow white I'm partial to bennies, reds, uppers, goofballs, jellies and Sudafed.

I won't touch Es – kid's stuff.

I'd be more than willing to try some of your stuff if it'll help you out.

I'll need the £70 as soon as we're done and you can keep the pic of my brain. I have absolutely no need for that whatsoever.

Let me know what time is good and the quality of gear you want me to test out.

Please get back to me as early as you can as I'll probably need to free up some appointments.

I run my own business.

Best regards

Ray

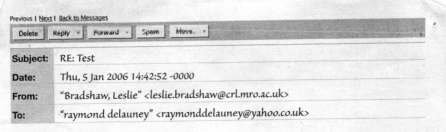

Delete   Reply   Forward   Spam   Move...

Subject:	RE: Test
Date:	Thu, 5 Jan 2006 14:42:52 -0000
From:	"Bradshaw, Leslie" <leslie.bradshaw@crl.mro.ac.uk>
To:	"raymond delauney" <raymonddelauney@yahoo.co.uk>

Hi Ray,

Thanks for your email – Can you email me your telephone number so I can conduct a screening questionnaire to see if you are eligible?

Many thanks,

Leslie

Delete   Reply   Forward   Spam   Move...

Date:	Thu, 5 Jan 2006 14:52:37 +0000 (GMT)
From:	"raymond delauney" <raymonddelauney@yahoo.co.uk>
Subject:	RE: Test
To:	"Bradshaw, Leslie" <leslie.bradshaw@crl.mro.ac.uk>

Hi Leslie,

I'm at work at the moment with clients in the vicinity.

I don't necessarily want them to eavesdrop on the nature of our conversation if you sniff what I'm smelling!

I'm pretty sure one of the guys here likes a bit of nosebag but I'm uncertain about Mikey, even if he does have dreads!

Just fire across the questionnaire and I'll knock it out over the next few mins as I'm chatting to them. I got a wall behind my PC so they won't smell a rat.

I'm eligible all right and know one bit of gear from another if you want me to rank and rate any of your stuff.

Cheers man,

Ray

Subject: RE: Test

Date: Thu, 5 Jan 2006 15:04:10 -0000

From: "Bradshaw, Leslie" <leslie.bradshaw@ crl.mro.ac.uk>

To: "raymond delauney" <raymonddelauney@yahoo.co.uk>

Hi Ray,

Ok, this is usually done over the phone so it may not be the easiest thing to fill out on the comp.

Many thanks,

Leslie

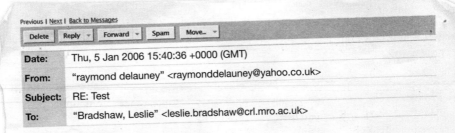

Previous | Next | Back to Messages

Delete   Reply   Forward   Spam   Move...

Date: Thu, 5 Jan 2006 15:40:36 +0000 (GMT)

From: "raymond delauney" <raymonddelauney@yahoo.co.uk>

Subject: RE: Test

To: "Bradshaw, Leslie" <leslie.bradshaw@crl.mro.ac.uk>

HI Leslie,

Thanks for sending me the form out.

My two clients are milling about, thinking about buying – if they overheard me talking drugs on the blower they may get the wrong idea and end up not buying. I'm sure you understand my need for privacy. I sell conservatories.

If you need one done we currently have a 22% off with our 'Conserve with a Conservatory' January sale. I could get you 25% off.

I'm doing pretty good but it's always nice to have an additional income.

I filled out everything in block capitals on the form and have attached it below.

Could you email a time and address I can come and try out the stuff you got.

Again, just to reiterate, I'm not keen on having a brain picture.

Thanks,

Ray

TELEPHONE SCREENING

We're investigating how levels of brain chemicals in people who've used Ecstasy compare to people who've used other or no drugs, and seeing if they have any effects on psychological performance.

Basically you'd spend one working day in the hospital, where you do two types of brain scan, and a couple of hours of psychological tests.

I'd like to ask you a few questions to see how you fit in with our research criteria, is that OK? All your answers are completely confidential, and please feel free to ask any questions you have.

Name   RAYMOND DELAUNEY
Date of Birth 28/04/1973
Age   32

Drug use history – I'm going to ask you a few questions about your drug use now. I'll go through some substances and ask you if you have used them, and how much.

	Ever Used? YES/ NO	When did you last use?	Regularly? How many years?	Days/month	Amount
MDMA or Ecstasy	No way	Tried once in 1990 maybe	Kid's stuff	no	no
Alcohol	All the time	Last night	Since 15	daily	10 pints + chasers

	Ever Used? YES/NO	When did you last use?	Regularly? How many years?	Days/month	Amount
Cannabis	Love it	Two nights ago – round Clarkeys	Since 17	weekly	Whatever's around
Cocaine	Very regular	Chopped on up last night	My fav drug big weakness	daily	Halved a line
Amphetamine	sure	Last week	Since 18 (late developer!)	weekly	Depends who's got what

Have you ever been a frequent user of any other drugs? – Which ones?
BENNIES, REDS, UPPERS, GOOFBALLS, JELLIES and SUDAFED

Has drug or alcohol use ever caused you problems? Ever treated?
NO MAJOR PROBLEMS – BAD DUMPS, STOMACH PAINS, HEADACHES – ALL MINOR

Have you ever injected any drug?
LEAVE IT OUT, MAN!

Psychiatric history – I'm going to ask you a few questions about your health now, remember, all your answers are completely confidential.

Have you ever experienced a period of time when you were feeling depressed or down most of the day, nearly every day?
OF COURSE – WHO HASN'T! SOME DAYS I FEEL LIKE CUTTING MYSELF UP WITH RAZOR BLADES OR THROWING MYSELF UNDER A TRAIN THAT IS MOVING BUT MOSTLY I'M HAPPY

…what about losing interest or pleasure in things you usually enjoy?
NAH, I'M PRETTY CONSISTENT. I LIKE FOOTBALL

Have you ever been diagnosed with depression or anxiety? What about any other psychiatric problem, like panic attacks?
I VERY RARELY GET PARA – EXCEPT WHEN I THINK SOMEONE'S NICKING MY GEAR OR CHATTING TO MY GIRL

Are you now, or have you ever had or been offered any treatment for depression, anxiety or any other psychiatric problem?

NEVER VISITED A SHRINK EVER – NOR DO I INTEND TO – THEY
ARE PRICEY

**Do any members of your immediate family have depression, anxiety or
any other psychiatric problem?**
MY FAMILY ARE WEIRDOS SO NOT THE BEST EXAMPLE. ONLY
ONE BROTHER LEFT ALIVE

**Are you currently taking any medication? Homeopathic/herbal? Head
injury?**
NO WAY MAN, THAT STUFF'S BAD FOR YOU

How much do you weigh? (Cannot be over 17.3 stone/110kg)
I'M WELL UNDER 12 STONE I HAVE TO RUN AROUND IN THE
SHOWER TO GET WET!

Have you had a brain scan before? PET scan?
NEVER HAD A BRAIN SCAN AND I HAVE NO PETS

Do you have a problem with needles?
NONE AT ALL

Are you very claustrophobic? Can you travel in a lift?
NO WORRIES THERE AT ALL. I LIKE LIFTS VERY MUCH

**Do you have any metal parts in your body? e.g. pins for broken bones etc.
Ever had an operation where something was implanted in your body?
metal worker, grinder, welder/shrapnel/tattoos on the head.**
NO METAL

Can jewellery/body piercing be removed?
WELL, SURE IT CAN

English first language??
YEAH

Can I explain a little more about it? Just before the scan the doctor will insert
a small needle into your arm. We then inject a chemical called a tracer (low
level radioactivity). This is a very small amount of radiation. (The total
radiation dose you will receive from the PET scans is about the same as you'd
receive in ten months living in the UK.) The scanner can then see how your
brain cells take up the chemical and how it leaves the brain again. You'd have
to lie still on the bed for 90mins with your head in the scanner. If you like we
can put the radio or CD on for you, while you lie there.
    The other type of scan we do is called an MRI. This uses radio waves
and a large magnet. It is not believed to have any hazards associated with it.

The MRI machine is enclosed, so people with bad claustrophobia may find it unacceptable.

Thank you very much. I'd like to send you some information sheets – very important you fully understand the procedures so please read carefully and think of any questions (can talk to a doctor if they want) – and also a questionnaire.

LISTEN, BABE, THE DOC CAN DO WHAT HE WANTS WITH ME – AS LONG AS I GET WEIGHED OUT STRAIGHT AFTER HIS EXPERIMENTS

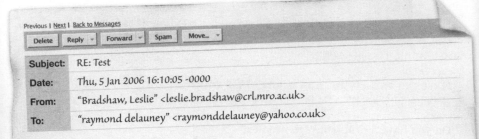

Previous | Next | Back to Messages

| Delete | Reply ▼ | Forward ▼ | Spam | Move... ▼ |

Subject:	RE: Test
Date:	Thu, 5 Jan 2006 16:10:05 -0000
From:	"Bradshaw, Leslie" <leslie.bradshaw@crl.mro.ac.uk>
To:	"raymond delauney" <raymonddelauney@yahoo.co.uk>

Hi Raymond,

Thanks for filling that out for me. Unfortunately, your cocaine use is slightly too high for us to use you in this project. We are looking for people who use it no more than 2x/week.

Sorry and thanks again for the time you spent – your details will be deleted.

Leslie

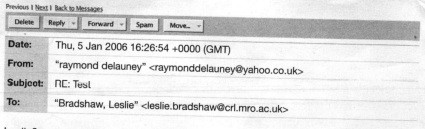

Previous | Next | Back to Messages

| Delete | Reply ▼ | Forward ▼ | Spam | Move... ▼ |

Date:	Thu, 5 Jan 2006 16:26:54 +0000 (GMT)
From:	"raymond delauney" <raymonddelauney@yahoo.co.uk>
Subject:	RE: Test
To:	"Bradshaw, Leslie" <leslie.bradshaw@crl.mro.ac.uk>

Leslie?

You're kidding me, right?

I thought you wanted people to be honest about their intake.

I know I put down a 'daily' intake under the snow white but the truth of the matter is I don't really earn enough for that. I usually take the stuff, say, twice a week.

I could use £70 right now for a little of the chop up. It's very moreish.

C'mon Leslie, I'll even share a Calvin Klein with you in the loo after we're done, please?

What if I re-hand the form in and cut down on the snort declaration?

I've just spent simply ages filling out the form.

One more try?

Ray

Previous | Next | Back to Messages

| Delete | Reply ▾ | Forward ▾ | Spam | Move... ▾ |

Subject:	RE: Test
Date:	Thu, 5 Jan 2006 16:30:04 -0000
From:	"Bradshaw, Leslie" <leslie.bradshaw@crl.mro.ac.uk>
To:	"raymond delauney" <raymonddelauney@yahoo.co.uk>

Hi Ray,

I'm really sorry that you spent time and we weren't able to use you, it would have been quicker over the phone – but that was your choice.

Anyway, I can't accept a new form as this is a serious medical trial. We are trying to establish the effects of certain drugs and we can not do so if we have an inaccurate record of drug use.

Sorry again,

Leslie

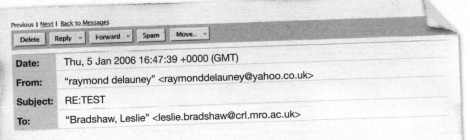

Previous | Next | Back to Messages

| Delete | Reply ▾ | Forward ▾ | Spam | Move... ▾ |

Date:	Thu, 5 Jan 2006 16:47:39 +0000 (GMT)
From:	"raymond delauney" <raymonddelauney@yahoo.co.uk>
Subject:	RE:TEST
To:	"Bradshaw, Leslie" <leslie.bradshaw@crl.mro.ac.uk>

Leslie,

Thanks very much.

Thanks for COMPLETELY WASTING MY TIME.

For TRYING TO GET ME SACKED BY TALKING ON THE PHONE ABOUT MY EXCESSIVE DRUG USE – all, as it turns out, for nothing.

How do I know you won't pass my name on to the Fuzz?

I think it's pathetic how people like you try and waste the time of ordinary, decent folk.

Anyway, I drop e bombs all the time. So stick that in your pipe and smoke it.

If ever you need a cheap conservatory don't even think about coming running to me with your tail in between your legs.

I suggest you scan your own brain. And further, I propose you employ the use of a high powered magnifying glass in trying to find it.

You absolute MESSER!

Raymond Delauney

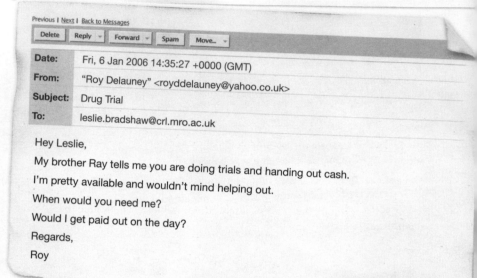

Previous | Next | Back to Messages

Delete Reply ▾ Forward ▾ Spam Move... ▾

Date:	Fri, 6 Jan 2006 14:35:27 +0000 (GMT)
From:	"Roy Delauney" <royddelauney@yahoo.co.uk>
Subject:	Drug Trial
To:	leslie.bradshaw@crl.mro.ac.uk

Hey Leslie,

My brother Ray tells me you are doing trials and handing out cash.

I'm pretty available and wouldn't mind helping out.

When would you need me?

Would I get paid out on the day?

Regards,

Roy

Previous | Next | Back to Messages

Delete Reply ▾ Forward ▾ Spam Move... ▾

Subject:	RE: Drug Trial
Date:	Fri, 6 Jan 2006 15:31:33 -0000
From:	"Bradshaw, Leslie" <leslie.bradshaw@crl.mro.ac.uk>
To:	"Roy Delauney" <royddelauney@yahoo.co.uk>

Hi Roy,

If you email me your number we can chat about this and go through a screening questionnaire to see if you are eligible.

We do not unfortunately, pay cash – we send out a cheque to all participants....

Many thanks,

Leslie

| Delete | Reply | Forward | Spam | Move... |

Date:	Fri, 6 Jan 2006 15:43:20 +0000 (GMT)
From:	"Roy Delauney" <royddelauney@yahoo.co.uk>
Subject:	RE: Drug Trial
To:	"Bradshaw, Leslie" <leslie.bradshaw@crl.mro.ac.uk>

Hi Leslie,

I'm still at work with a lot of people looking at discounted conservatories.

Can you email it through again.

Thanks,

Roy

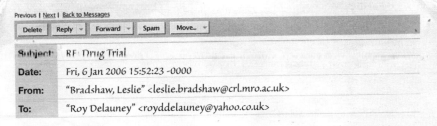

| Delete | Reply | Forward | Spam | Move... |

Subject:	RE: Drug Trial
Date:	Fri, 6 Jan 2006 15:52:23 -0000
From:	"Bradshaw, Leslie" <leslie.bradshaw@crl.mro.ac.uk>
To:	"Roy Delauney" <royddelauney@yahoo.co.uk>

Hi Roy,

Thanks for your enquiry but unfortunately I don't think we will be able to use you in this project.

Kind regards,

Leslie

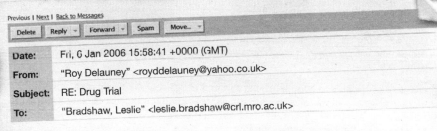

| Delete | Reply | Forward | Spam | Move... |

Date:	Fri, 6 Jan 2006 15:58:41 +0000 (GMT)
From:	"Roy Delauney" <royddelauney@yahoo.co.uk>
Subject:	RE: Drug Trial
To:	"Bradshaw, Leslie" <leslie.bradshaw@crl.mro.ac.uk>

Leslie,

What have you got against us Delauneys? First you waste my brother, Roy's time and now mine.

I am very keen to participate.

I can turn up anytime you want, man.

Could you please make the cheque payable to R. Delauney.

Roy

END OF CORRESPONDENCE

TRAMPOLINE

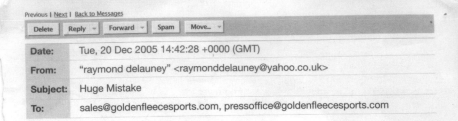

| Delete | Reply ▾ | Forward ▾ | Spam | Move... ▾ |

Date:	Tue, 20 Dec 2005 14:42:28 +0000 (GMT)
From:	"raymond delauney" <raymonddelauney@yahoo.co.uk>
Subject:	Huge Mistake
To:	sales@goldenfleecesports.com, pressoffice@goldenfleecesports.com

Dear Sir/Madam

I write to you having just endured one of the most traumatic weeks of my life. A situation I blame solely on your firm and in particular the contraption you market, namely the Bigger Bounce trampoline.

I am in England on vacation from Wisconsin to see my sister and her young family over the festive period.

I purchased the Bigger Bounce as a Christmas present for my nephew with the intention of getting him out of the house and doing a bit of exercise.

Sadly Acer (who is 12) belongs to what I term the 'fat kid' generation. That is to say, children who prefer playing computer games and stuffing their fat faces rather than going out in the back yard and playing ball.

I've told his mom time and time again that she should urgently begin to address Acer's obesity before it becomes a serious health concern. My ass of a sister simply tries to hush me up and change the subject, as if the blubber will magically disappear all by itself.

A typical example of bad parenting.

Acer's way of responding to my warnings is to start bawling uncontrollably before waddling up to his room, presumably to munch on another candy bar. I yell after him that turning a blind eye to his tubbiness will not solve the issue but my pleas fall on fat ears.

I've sat Acer down and offered to send him to 'Fat School,' at my expense, however he seems quite content to continue his obese ways and run the risk of encountering heart trouble in later life. Ultimately, I guess, it's his call. I've lost one family member to fatness. I sure don't want to lose another.

To the matter in hand:

Attempting to find a fun solution to helping Acer drop some pounds I bought the Bigger Bounce.

I decided to try out the device for myself, primarily to ensure its suitability for an overweight 12-year-old.

The weather was particularly unforgiving on that day so I thought I'd try a preliminary bounce in the front room to test out the device. Please note that nowhere on the item does it warn "Not to be used indoors".

Initially I was fairly pleased with the springiness of the mat. Unfortunately I was completely unaware of the extreme peril I had placed myself in. I managed to successfully negotiate one somersault to the amused applause of my wife before the inevitable disaster struck.

I hardly exerted any downward pressure of note yet I was hurled skywards at the speed of a bullet being released by a high-powered rifle, say an AK-47.

My flight was prematurely and painfully interrupted by the immovable presence of the ceiling. My wife could only look on in horror as she watched my head peel open and spray the artex a shocking stain of red before entering my descent on a horizontal trajectory, fracturing my left ankle on landing.

My wife immediately summoned the London Ambulance service on her cell phone. They were slow to arrive and once at the scene, seemed indifferent to the severe nature of my injuries.

One thing was apparent – the incredulous look on both their faces when I told them that your product bore no warning of excessive springiness and no mention not to use it in an indoor capacity. They just looked at each other in their lime green uniforms and shook their heads like they couldn't believe what they were hearing. I'd be mightily surprised if I was the only person suffering head injuries from the result of interaction with your product here in the UK.

I have attached a photo of the damage done to the front room ceiling, which I will have to now pay to repair. I have had to have 12 stitches inserted in my head; I can attach a photo of my bandaged head and a comprehensive hospital report detailing the full extent of my injuries. My short-term memory has been adversely affected.

Thanks to the Bigger Bounce I will be spending this Xmas in plaster. I intend to initiate a lawsuit to compensate for loss of earnings through injury and also to cover the cost of the damage done to the ceiling, and myself, as and when I regain the use of my legs.

Can you please inform me how you intend to go about recompensing me?

I have a receipt of purchase.

I await an apology and an explanation.

I should add my short-term memory has also been adversely affected.

Raymond Delauney

Subject:	RE: Huge Mistake
Date:	Tue, 20 Dec 2005 15:14:19 -0000
From:	"GF Sports (Thomas Dove)" <thomas@goldenfleecesports.com>
To:	"raymond delauney" <raymonddelauney@yahoo.co.uk>

Dear Mr Delauney

Sorry to hear of your "accident". However, I cannot find any of your order information and as such I cannot react to your situation.

Please supply me with details of your order address and contact number so I can speak with you personally.

Best regards,

Thomas Dove

Golden Fleece Sports

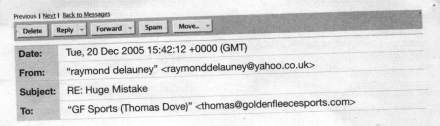

Date:	Tue, 20 Dec 2005 15:42:12 +0000 (GMT)
From:	"raymond delauney" <raymonddelauney@yahoo.co.uk>
Subject:	RE: Huge Mistake
To:	"GF Sports (Thomas Dove)" <thomas@goldenfleecesports.com>

Dove,

Firstly why in hell's name have you wrapped the word 'accident' in inverted commas?

Do you seriously think I would injure myself on purpose?

Is that what you are implying, buster?

You complete clot.

I can do without any attitude, fat ass. I can come down on you very hard and close this ramshackle business down if I choose to. So show me a little courtesy here, bozo.

My wife paid for the death trap contraption – not me.

Her name is Richelle Rogers, she is an actor.

Run that through the computer, smart ass.

Never mind order numbers, how are you going to compensate me?

You better get your dunce's cap off and your thinking one on sonny Jim or I'm going to get IRATE.

Raymond Delauney

Delete   Reply ▼   Forward ▼   Spam   Move... ▼

Subject:	Trampoline Incident
Date:	Wed, 21 Dec 2005 11:00:29 -0000
From:	"Clare Boone" <Clare@goldenfleecesports.com>
To:	raymonddelauney@yahoo.co.uk

Dear Mr Delauney

Thank you for your recent correspondence. To enable me to deal with your complaint correctly I will need a copy of your receipt and your full address. I look forward to hearing from you shortly.

Many thanks

Clare Boone

Customer Relations

Incident Management

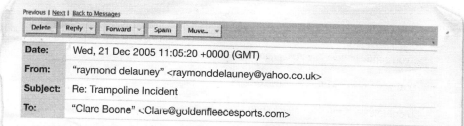

Delete   Reply ▼   Forward ▼   Spam   Move... ▼

Date:	Wed, 21 Dec 2005 11:05:20 +0000 (GMT)
From:	"raymond delauney" <raymonddelauney@yahoo.co.uk>
Subject:	Re: Trampoline Incident
To:	"Clare Boone" <Clare@goldenfleecesports.com>

What incident? I know not of what you speak and to be perfectly honest I have my hands full with trying to repair a hole in my ceiling.

God knows how it got there.

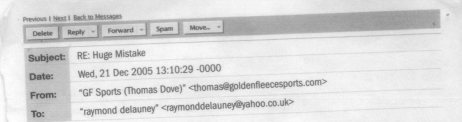

Delete | Reply ▼ | Forward ▼ | Spam | Move... ▼

Subject:	RE: Huge Mistake
Date:	Wed, 21 Dec 2005 13:10:29 -0000
From:	"GF Sports (Thomas Dove)" <thomas@goldenfleecesports.com>
To:	"raymond delauney" <raymonddelauney@yahoo.co.uk>

We take these comments very seriously, however, what I do not understand is how several UK retailers have received the same email? As such, the UK distribution company for Bigger Bounce products are currently seeking further information to ensure any future litigation would be suitably founded.

I would kindly ask you to supply me with a contact phone number so we can speak in person.

Have a merry Christmas.

Best regards,

Thomas Dove

Delete | Reply ▼ | Forward ▼ | Spam | Move... ▼

Date:	Wed, 21 Dec 2005 11:29:33 +0000 (GMT)
From:	"raymond delauney" <raymonddelauney@yahoo.co.uk>
Subject:	Re: FW: Huge Mistake
To:	"GF Sports (Thomas Dove)" <thomas@goldenfleecesports.com>

Hello Mr Dove,

I have absolutely no clue as to who you are, what you want from me or what garbage it is you are selling.

Is this Bigger Bounce some sort of todger enhancing drug? If so, I am simply not interested.

I once purchased some cream that claimed it would magically make my manhood bigger. It had no effect whatsoever.

When I thought about it some more, I realized if it actually did work I would have massive hands, which is something I really could do without.

Bloody ludicrous.

Raymond

Subject:	RE: Huge Mistake
Date:	Wed, 21 Dec 2005 13:10:29 -0000
From:	"GF Sports (Thomas Dove)" <thomas@goldenfleecesports.com>
To:	"raymond delauney" <raymonddelauney@yahoo.co.uk>

I am selling you absolutely nothing.

You approached us and several other UK retailers with your original correspondence.

I do not take kindly to receiving mail that slanders the products that we sell and results in a complete waste of energy from both myself and other colleagues. The brand you have questioned is globally recognised and the relevant authorities have been made aware of the comments you have made.

I would suggest a retraction is made by you regarding the brand in question with the utmost haste.

Best regards,

Thomas Dove

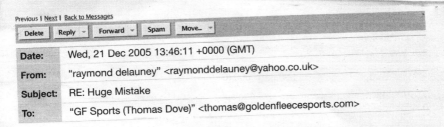

Date:	Wed, 21 Dec 2005 13:46:11 +0000 (GMT)
From:	"raymond delauney" <raymonddelauney@yahoo.co.uk>
Subject:	RE: Huge Mistake
To:	"GF Sports (Thomas Dove)" <thomas@goldenfleecesports.com>

Dove,

I am simply not interested in anything you have to sell me so you might as well stop hassling me.

As for your laughable claim that I have wasted your energy, well frankly, it made me laugh. Once I stopped laughing, I started laughing some more.

I very much doubt you've a day's work inside you and if you had any particle of gumption you'd hardly be heading up the Trampoline Enquiries section of Golden Fleece Sports. Where does the next promotion take you? Swingball Returns perhaps?

Please stop pestering me. Christmas is coming and I intend to enjoy it.

Merry Xmas

Raymond Delauney

END OF CORRESPONDENCE

DELAUNEY UNTO HIMSELF ADVERTISING

Delete   Reply ▾   Forward ▾   Spam   Move... ▾

Date:	Fri, 3 Feb 2006 12:10:07 +0000 (GMT)
From:	"raymond delauney" <raymonddelauney@yahoo.co.uk>
Subject:	Top TV Advert Writer
To:	"Jonathan Gold" <jgold@goodideateam.com>

Hi,

Did you see what it said on the subject heading?

Yeah, well I am what it says on the label, to coin the phrase of some other advert.

Quite simply, I am a superbly gifted TV writer. I have a special skill for seeing what the public desire and tapping into that vein of 'want'.

You guys seem to be making pots of money. Pretty impressive. I bet you've got a huge office and a couple of tasty looking PA's.

So have I.

I have just formed a brand new start up – my very own Advertising Agency – and it will be absolutely huge. I have an aggressive four-year business plan that will see me locking horns with the likes of Saatchi in Year 3.

I have something I might be able to chuck your way.

I'm a fiercely individual talent who prefers to work alone as my artistic temperament inevitably leads to personality clashes with bosses who know far less than I.

At my last job I was hailed a "genius" in the morning and then described as the "most deluded individual I have ever had the misfortune to meet" by the same person on the very same day. I was later sacked.

So I decided to branch out alone and assemble a dedicated team of talented writers I could sack should any dare to disagree with me. I work from the confines of my own home where I can't rub anyone up the wrong way.

I'm not inexpensive but you'll get great value for money.

I'm after your account and below is a sample of what my team of copywriters can produce at short notice.

TV ADVERT

The Product is **Minstrels**, the creamy milk chocolate in a crisp shell from **Galaxy**.

Husband (watching football on TV): Can I fix you a cup of tea, baby doll?

Wife (looking miserable with towel wrapped round head): I don't want any tea.

Husband: I'll put those shelves up later on today.

Wife: No rush, it's taken you 4 years to get this far.

Husband: Throws wife a bumper packet of Minstrels

(Camera zooms in on wife's changing expression)

Wife: Starts smiling

Voice Over: **"Don't Suffer from Pre Minstrel Tension"**

Galaxy is running this campaign in the summer with 4 variants on the theme.

I have this copyrighted so nicking it would be an expensive error. I'll be blunt. I want to do business with you.

Get back to me at your earliest convenience and I'll see what my team can create for you.

If you want me to apply my skills to any work on a trial basis I'll be more than happy to do so at a reduced rate.

Best regards,

Raymond Delauney

Delauney Unto Himself Innovative Advertising Ltd

Previous | Next | Back to Messages

Delete   Reply ▾   Forward ▾   Spam   Move... ▾

Subject:	RE: Top TV Advert Writer
Date:	Mon, 6 Feb 2006 20:17:18 -0500
From:	"Jonathan Gold" <jgold@goodideateam.com>
To:	"raymond delauney" <raymonddelauney@yahoo.co.uk>

Hi Raymond:

Many thanks for your inquiry and very humorous message.

I want to acknowledge receipt of your message; as a director of content here, I don't have any direct uses for your talent at this time, but will keep you on file as we may determine we need some concepting/storyboarding done.

However, several other executives here also got your message, and you may hear from them independent of me.

Meanwhile, I could def. relate to your story, which, BTW, could make for a hilarious, yet realistic movie of this kind of work (if it makes you feel any better, I also have been declared an amazing genius only to be fired for the same ability: my conclusion: geniuses are lonely).

Also, as we are focusing on high-end ad agencies, my sales people may be contacting you for some feedback as well.

Best of luck with your own company.

Jonathan Gold

Sr. Director

Previous | Next | Back to Messages

| Delete | Reply ▾ | Forward ▾ | Spam | Move... ▾ |

Date:	Tue, 7 Feb 2006 12:48:39 +0000 (GMT)
From:	"raymond delauney" <raymonddelauney@yahoo.co.uk>
Subject:	RE: Top TV Advert Writer
To:	"Jonathan Gold" <jgold@goodideateam.com>

Jonathan,

Many thanks for replying to my mail. I was disappointed to learn that there are 'no direct uses of my talent at this time'. However, I feel suitably encouraged that you recognise and respect my unmistakable flair and look forward to working with you on any 'indirect' opportunities as and when they may arise.

I'm encouraged too that you are of my ilk, tis a rare breed we belong to, my similarly gifted friend. Of course, the old playground adage may well apply, 'it takes one to know one'.

Apparently Einstein's brain was so overworked thinking up fiendishly clever equations that little inconsequential details like putting on a pair of trousers occasionally eschewed his attention. I bet when he wandered down the high street minus his pantaloons not many people remarked, 'Look at that genius over there.' They just saw a man with unruly hair in underpants. So few people possess vision these days.

So, after being sacked I decided to start up my own business, slap on it a silly name, bestow on myself the most impressive of titles and recruit talented people, pretty much like myself, except of course they will be earning a considerably smaller salary.

The interviewing process was fun. I posed questions, I offered scenarios, I acted strangely, I argued and hilariously, I insulted pretty much everyone I interviewed – without exception.

I opened up one interview by studiously looking at the applicant's resume before saying, "Why are you wasting my time?" He's now working for me, the silly fool. Another interview was conducted with a pair of underpants over my head – the girl initially looked surprised but made no reference at any stage to the misplaced underwear – and nor did I.

At one point, midway through one interview, my secretary brought in the plate of drawing pins and raisins I had 'asked for'. I took a drawing pin put it in my mouth and offered the plate to the applicant who took and ate a raisin. Doubtless he thought this to be some sort of isometric test and not the playful antics of a mischievous fool.

I was and am looking for individualism and, above all, the ability to look at the world in different ways, to question and challenge accepted notions.

I hope our professional paths cross again at some point.

I feel sure they shall.

Best regards,

Raymond

Delauney Unto Himself Advertising

END OF CORRESPONDENCE

BARRY HEARN AND 'SLIM'

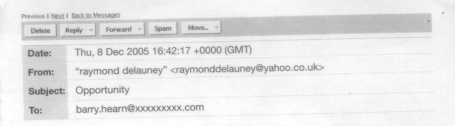

| Delete | Reply ▾ | Forward ▾ | Spam | Move... ▾ |

Date:	Thu, 8 Dec 2005 16:42:17 +0000 (GMT)
From:	"raymond delauney" <raymonddelauney@yahoo.co.uk>
Subject:	Opportunity
To:	barry.hearn@xxxxxxxxx.com

Barry

I've been a fight fan ever since I was a kid, I could mix it in the squared circle pretty good myself and if I wasn't so talented in other areas I might have become the first white heavyweight champion since the great Rocky Balboa, game as a pebble was Rocky.

I write to you as one successful businessman to another. Like you I've got to the top of my field through sheer hard work and bloody-minded determination.

I got something I can put your way. Something you might need now that the milking exercise on the cash cow that is Steve Davis is drying up. No offence.

This crackpot Government actually want us to work up to age 67. Not me, Barry, I plan to be swanning about in my villa in Tenerife drinking something fizzy and strumping cocktail waitresses ten to the dozen.

I was raised in Canning Town in the east end of London, a place you probably know well as it houses the famous Peacock gym. I can tell you back in the days when I was a street urchin there was just as much fighting outside that place as there was in – a lion escaped from the local zoo once – and four kids mauled it to death!

If you wanted something nice the only way to get it was to work hard – or nick it. I chose to work hard, mostly. Okay, during the early part of my career I may have conned a few people along the way. Who hasn't?

And that's why I respect you – you're a grafter same as me. Muscling in on a cartel of boxing promoters ain't for the lily livered.

As we're cut from the same working class cloth I'm not going to flannel you or use any 'rope a dope' tactics to snare you with. Not that you're a dope.

I confess the first part of this mail is what's known as the 'butter up'. A standard sales procedure employed by the very best salesmen the aim of which is to establish a common point of interest and make any subsequent buyer feel friendlier towards you. You can't beat a bit of butter.

I know how to manipulate a market, and believe me when I say when it comes to selling I'm the best in the business. The Sugar Ray of Sales.

Boy, I can sell. Someone once asked me what the definition of a good salesman is. I'll tell you – a sharp talker who can sell something to someone that that person doesn't want. I've sold all sorts of shit to people, stuff they didn't need, didn't want or couldn't afford.

I started out selling scams (you can't con an honest man I always say) then graduated to windows (I glazed most of Essex), jewellery (worthless bling at big prices), Hoovers (every house has a Hoover), timeshare (time to share their money).

You name it I've flogged it to people who've shook my hand with a smile after I've stitched them up.

There's nobody better than me, not at selling, Baz and I'd like to tell you my very next sale will be to you. It's going to be something you are going to want and something that will make you a lot of money.

So you want to know what it is, right? Hold your horses.

No doubt you are aware of Michael Buffer.

The Yank ring announcer with the orange face and the barnet that looks like he has three people working on it full time.

This chump has trademarked the phrase "Let's get ready to rumble."

If someone told me this guy gets flown all over the world and paid millions for a few minutes on a microphone I'd think they were crazy. But it's true.

My mission was to unearth a British equivalent and I have tracked him down.

His name is James Dip but everyone knows him as Slim Jim or Skinny Dip.

Slim weighs in at around about 30 stone and used to sing in the Welsh male choir. He's got a big booming velvet voice the like of which you've never heard before. He makes Tom Jones sound like a soprano whose balls haven't yet descended.

Slim almost has as much personality as he does flab. I'm telling you this boy will become a legend in the boxing game. The crowds love him.

He can do a little tap as well and has a funny dance he can do to the Kung Foo fighting song.

I'm working on a catchphrase to compete with the 'rumble' one. I think Slim needs a gimmick. We could just go for something straightforward and no nonsense like,

"Let's have a fucking tear up."

I'm offering you first refusal on this one Barry, I've always preferred you to Frank Warren.

I've got Slim signed up on contract. You could buy it off me or hire him. I'm open to offers. We could both cream off Slim for a good few years.

Let me know your initial thoughts.

Best regards

Raymond Delauney

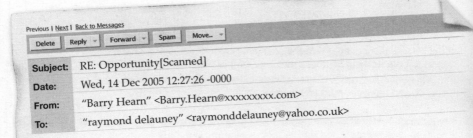

Previous | Next | Back to Messages

Delete	Reply ⌄	Forward ⌄	Spam	Move... ⌄

Subject:	RE: Opportunity[Scanned]
Date:	Wed, 14 Dec 2005 12:27:26 -0000
From:	"Barry Hearn" <Barry.Hearn@xxxxxxxxx.com>
To:	"raymond delauney" <raymonddelauney@yahoo.co.uk>

Dear Raymond,

Great email! I am sorry, but I do have a long-term contract with John McDonald, so therefore have no room for 'Slim'.

Best regards,

Barry

END OF CORRESPONDENCE

SPORTS REPORTER JOB APPLICATION

Delete | Reply ▾ | Forward ▾ | Spam | Move... ▾

Date: Tue, 19 Dec 2006 12:26:23 +0000 (GMT)

From: "raymond delauney" <raymonddelauney@yahoo.co.uk>

Subject: Top Sports Reporter

To: lreeves@dlsworld.com

Hi Lily,

I became aware of your advertisement for sports reporters late last week. I really think you could do worse than take a long hard look at me.

I'm uncertain of the exact criteria you are looking for – but if it's a top drawer sports reporter blessed with a flamboyant streak, an investigative nose and all round creative genius, then wham bam – I'm very much your man.

I've got shit loads of experience under my belt and a solid grasp of the French language. I also speak conversational Swedish.

My football knowledge is encyclopaedic, I churn out copy at will and can work inside any realistic deadline you care to set. I prefer to plough my own furrow, away from the common clichéd herd. I'm not one of those bland hacks who gets copy in after it's needed. I deliver what you want when you bloody well want it.

In short, I'm an awesome writer.

I've two more distinctive characteristics I think it's only fair to mention. I'm a grafter and a straight shooter. By that I mean I tell it how it is. You'll always know where you stand with me whether you like it or not. I'm a senior writer; accordingly I expect to be treated like one.

I'll spell one thing now. Subs do not and will not alter a word of my copy. There are those who can write and those who add or delete commas. I've had plenty of stand up rows with many a sub including, many years ago, a right old tear up in the car park over the validity of a split infinitive.

I'm altogether calmer these days but still feel passionately that subs shouldn't meddle with the sort of crafted copy they themselves are wholly incapable of producing.

I've worked for national titles, lifestyle magazines and a whole host of local rags.

Two questions:

How much are you paying and when would you need me to start?
Where are you based? I'm free anytime this week before Xmas for an interview.

I can dust down my CV and fizz it through at will but would ideally prefer a vis a vis (face to face) chat to discuss how you would benefit from my services and what you would be prepared to offer me.

If you so wish I am more than prepared to submit trial copy on ANY subject you wish.

It will sparkle.

Regards,

Raymond Delauney

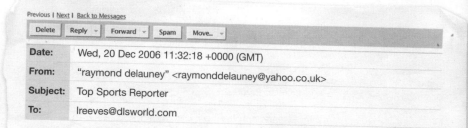

Previous | Next | Back to Messages

Delete | Reply | Forward | Spam | Move...

Date:	Wed, 20 Dec 2006 11:32:18 +0000 (GMT)
From:	"raymond delauney" <raymonddelauney@yahoo.co.uk>
Subject:	Top Sports Reporter
To:	lreeves@dlsworld.com

I sent this through already and would appreciate a response whether it be positive or negative.

Thanks,

Ray

Previous | Next | Back to Messages

Delete | Reply | Forward | Spam | Move...

Subject:	RE: Top Sports Reporter
Date:	Wed, 20 Dec 2006 11:40:57 -0000
From:	"Reeves, Lorena" <lreeves@dlsworld.com>
To:	"raymond delauney" <raymonddelauney@yahoo.co.uk>

Positive – it's the funniest email I've had all year. Incidentally if your football knowledge really is encyclopaedic –

Which British footballer has played for four teams that have won the European Cup but has never won it himself?

Lorena

Lily,

Not exactly sure what amused you in my mail but I appreciate the swiftness of your mail (after my prompt) all the same.

Is the question the interview? Is it the toughest test you could come up with?

At the risk of sounding patronising (that's when you talk down to people) when I said my knowledge of the game is encyclopaedic I damn well meant it.

From memory I couldn't think of one player who has played for four different clubs that have won the European Cup but never won it himself. I could think of three.

Dean Saunders – Liverpool, Nottingham Forest, Aston Villa and Benfica
Ronaldo – PSV Eindhoven, Barcelona, Inter Milan, Real Madrid
Pierre Van Hooijdonk – Celtic, Forest, Benfica, Feyenoord

Listen, you sound like an intelligent woman. The next step from here is to hire me – at a fancy salary. I suggest you contact your superiors and tell 'em you got a major transfer target for the January window but you might have to break the bank to land him.

It'll be worth it.

Every team needs a superstar and, to be brutally frank, it's me in't it?

Hey, and while you're chewing on that, I got one for you.

Who is the only current Premiership player to have won the Champions League, UEFA Cup, Premiership and FA Cup?

It's lemon squeasy for me but let's see how you fare, sunshine.

Relentlessly,

Raymond Delauney

Nwanku Kanu?

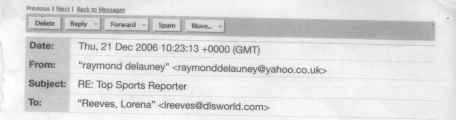

Delete   Reply ▾   Forward ▾   Spam   Move... ▾

Date:	Thu, 21 Dec 2006 10:23:13 +0000 (GMT)
From:	"raymond delauney" <raymonddelauney@yahoo.co.uk>
Subject:	RE: Top Sports Reporter
To:	"Reeves, Lorena" <lreeves@dlsworld.com>

Lily/Lorena,

How come you're now addressing yourself as Lorena?

Anyway, whatever you choose to call yourself congratulations to whoever handed you the answer.

Let's get down to brass tacks:

How much are you guys gonna tempt me with? I drive a hard bargain but I'm sure we can come to some sort of compromise.

How about £60k? That's my opening gambit.

Raymond Delauney

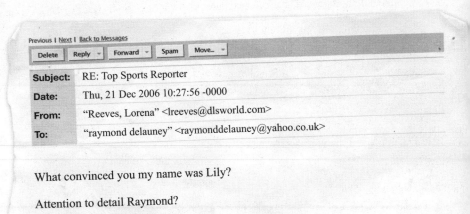

Delete   Reply ▾   Forward ▾   Spam   Move... ▾

Subject:	RE: Top Sports Reporter
Date:	Thu, 21 Dec 2006 10:27:56 -0000
From:	"Reeves, Lorena" <lreeves@dlsworld.com>
To:	"raymond delauney" <raymonddelauney@yahoo.co.uk>

What convinced you my name was Lily?

Attention to detail Raymond?

It's a requirement of the job I'm afraid.

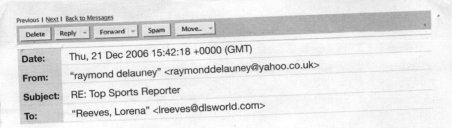

Delete   Reply ▾   Forward ▾   Spam   Move... ▾

Date:	Thu, 21 Dec 2006 15:42:18 +0000 (GMT)
From:	"raymond delauney" <raymonddelauney@yahoo.co.uk>
Subject:	RE: Top Sports Reporter
To:	"Reeves, Lorena" <lreeves@dlsworld.com>

Okay Lorena,

The interchange of emails, the sparring, your palpable appreciation of me – it's time to hold fire.

I think you could use a guy like me. I mean, in a professional capacity. I think you know that.

The good news is I'm available. There is no bad news.

The ball, as they say, is very much on your side of the court.

Raymond

Delete   Reply ▾   Forward ▾   Spam   Move... ▾

Subject:	RE: Top Sports Reporter
Date:	Fri, 22 Dec 2006 11:23:33 -0000
From:	"Reeves, Lorena" <lreeves@dlsworld.com>
To:	"raymond delauney" <raymonddelauney@yahoo.co.uk>

Dear Raymond

Your emails have made my Christmas but I'm afraid the position has now been filled.

All the best,

Lorena

END OF CORRESPONDENCE

PR AGENCY JOB APPLICATION

Competitive salary, central London

One of the UK's leading broadcast PR agencies is looking for two motivated, talented and enthusiastic individuals to join its busy media team.

SMDdemand provides radio, TV and online journalists with several stories and interviews every day. The campaigns are many and varied, from government departments and charities to consumer brands and sporting organisations. The atmosphere is fast paced, fun and challenging.

We want a fourth member of the radio forward planning team who brief producers, presenters and newsroom journalists about the latest stories and features. The right candidate will need to know what 'works' on radio, how to spot a story and have excellent phone skills.

Only those with the ability to write a concise and attention grabbing press release coupled with an excellent phone manner need apply for either position. Knowledge of the UK broadcast market and how the media works is highly desirable so applications from radio journalists and PR professionals are welcomed.

No agencies please.

Previous I Next I Back to Messages

| Delete | Reply ▾ | Forward ▾ | Spam | Move... ▾ |

Date:	Wed, 10 Jan 2007 21:47:32 +0000 (GMT)
From:	"raymond delauney" <raymonddelauney@yahoo.co.uk>
Subject:	Job Advertisement
To:	GWynn@SMDdemand.com

Hello,

I've seen your advertisement for motivated, talented and enthusiastic individuals. I'm very probably the person you are looking for.

The problem is this: I've endured an exhausting day searching for work on websites so when I finally see a vacancy matching my skills I'd really like to know what (or how much) is being offered in return.

This is ever such an important piece of information that helps me decide whether I'd be interested in the job or not.

I let you benefit from my skill sets, you pay me. That's pretty much how the worker/ employer relationship works.

Your company would benefit enormously by hiring me. I know what 'works' on radio and I know what doesn't (Chris Evans, for example).

Frankly though I'm a little suspicious about the need for an "excellent phone manner". Just as "cuddly" translates to obese in dating ads, "excellent phone manner" in job descriptions generally decodes to cold calling people and then selling them some crap.

One last observation: I've worked for several firms all of which would describe their workplace as "fast paced, fun and challenging". Without exception they haven't been, not for the employee at any rate.

I consider it a little ironic that you require someone to create original attention grabbing prose when your advert is (frankly) a jargonised, clichéd mess.

Having said all that, I haven't entirely ruled out the existence of a possible working relationship. I'm an outstanding writer and right now I'm out of work after I let my former boss in on a few home truths.

If you get back to me swiftly with an exact figure pertaining to the salary, I'll have a clearer idea as to whether or not I'd be interested in working with you.

Best regards,

Raymond Delauney

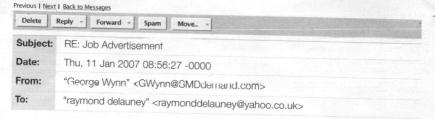

| Delete | Reply ⌄ | Forward ⌄ | Spam | Move... ⌄ |

Subject:	RE: Job Advertisement
Date:	Thu, 11 Jan 2007 08:56:27 -0000
From:	"George Wynn" <GWynn@SMDdemand.com>
To:	"raymond delauney" <raymonddelauney@yahoo.co.uk>

Hi Raymond

Thank you for your considered email, which I read with interest this morning. I'm sorry to hear about your exhausting day yesterday, hopefully today will be less tiring for you.

Thank you too for your insight into the world of work – absolute genius ('I let you benefit from my skill sets, you pay me' – although I would say that 'benefit' is probably stretching it a bit).

But let's get down to the nitty gritty. With regards to salary I'd be happy to pay you the sum total of £0 pa if you would be prepared to come to work here, sell some 'crap' and tell me some home truths.

But let's lose the annoyingly smug tone you've decided to adopt. Unlike yourself I unfortunately have ruled out a working relationship with you and I'd ask you not to waste my time in future with tedious emails like this. Having said that I sincerely hope that you apply for every other job in this manner.

Warmest wishes

George

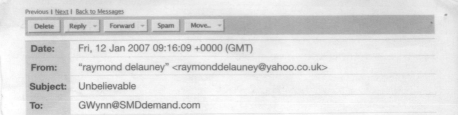

| Delete | Reply ⌄ | Forward ⌄ | Spam | Move... ⌄ |

Date:	Fri, 12 Jan 2007 09:16:09 +0000 (GMT)
From:	"raymond delauney" <raymonddelauney@yahoo.co.uk>
Subject:	Unbelievable
To:	GWynn@SMDdemand.com

George,

After returning home in jovial mood from a fun day paintballing my disposition took a distinct turn for the worse after reading your embittered, mean spirited mail.

Clearly in your position as a minor marketing monkey you have nothing better to do than be palpably rude to those people good natured enough to offer you constructive criticism.

Your abject attitude is something I refuse to accept. I don't think there is any way I would be prepared to attend an interview now, even if you were to offer a grovelling apology.

Forget the nitty gritty. Let's get down to brass tacks.

I was educated at an undistinguished public school, represented Peterborough U14's as a National Schools ABA finalist and achieved a First Class Honours degree at Cambridge (Screen Media and Cultures).

My dissertation covered the Japanese Gangster/Yakuza Film (from Kurosawa to Kitano) to widespread critical acclaim and may soon be published.

I have further work experience at the British Film Institute library and Superdrug.

I'd say that makes me smarter than you, a whole lot smarter.

Where do you go from here?

I would suggest you issue me an unreserved apology – in addition to an unequivocal assurance that all further job advertisements will (clearly) stipulate full details of salaries on offer (including benefits).

Otherwise I may have to draw attention to your gross ineptitude to your immediate superior, the head cleaner.

Yours relentlessly,

Raymond Delauney

END OF CORRESPONDENCE

LEAFLETING

Date:	Fri, 7 Jul 2006 22:10:55 +0100 (BST)
From:	"raymond delauney" <raymonddelauney@yahoo.co.uk>
Subject:	Top Leafleter
To:	luke@topstuffpromotions.com

Hi,

I'll do the job of leafleting you are advertising. I am experienced in this field, very reliable and British. I think it helps if you speak the language in case anyone asks you a question about whatever you are advertising.

Bad leafleters just stand there and hand out leaflets – a good one will make out he's enjoying it.

I have handed out cheap telephone cards before. Even during the cold weather people took their hands out of their pockets to take a card. I sometimes follow them for a few yards so they don't chuck it in the nearest bin – that way it will end up in their pocket.

I'm also prepared to stand around with a very big sign if you want. I've done it for Subway.

I'm trying to raise enough money to put myself through night school. Leafleting isn't a long term goal for me.

Does anyone check up to see if you are handing the leaflets out?

I was only asking because some people are dumpers. I'm not – you can rest assured of that.

Please let me know if you want me to pop along for an interview.

Best regards,

Raymond Delauney

Delete   Reply ▾   Forward ▾   Spam   Move... ▾

From:	"Luke Poole" <luke@topstuffpromotions.com>
Subject:	Re: Top Leafleter
Date:	Sat, 8 Jul 2006 17:01:05 +0100
To:	"raymond delauney" <raymonddelauney@yahoo.co.uk>

Hi Raymond,

Please can you supply a contact number.

Many thanks.

Luke Poole
Top Stuff Promotions Limited

Delete   Reply ▾   Forward ▾   Spam   Move... ▾

Date:	Mon, 10 Jul 2006 18:29:23 +0100 (BST)
From:	"raymond delauney" <raymonddelauney@yahoo.co.uk>
Subject:	Re: Top Leafleter
To:	"Luke Poole" <luke@topstuffpromotions.com>

Lukey,

Thanks for getting back to me.

I would have responded sooner but Net Profit the nearest internet cafe to me in Acton have decided to hike their prices up from 50 pence an hour to £1 every half hour without telling anyone about it.

I only had 50 pence on me, Saturday and some camp looking bloke on the till started screaming at me in front of a whole load of people, mainly Australians. In the end I said I'd give it to him later but I'm never going back because he made me look an idiot.

I've had my phone stolen last week – with £8 pre-pay on it! – Have you a personal line I can call you on?

I'm working for Subway at present holding a big sign and handing out leaflets. I get about 3 people every day who think they're really funny by asking if I know where the nearest Subway is whilst I'm holding a 6 foot Subway sign.

It's not even funny the first time.

Can you match £4 an hour – cash?

I can do any day except every other Friday at 11am and even then I'd be available in the afternoon. I also get a free sandwich so if you guys want to throw a bit extra to cover lunch in I'd definitely be interested.

I'd also be interested in any office work such as filing or photocopying things. Got to go as only have three mins left.

Best regards,

Raymond

Previous | Next | Back to Messages

Delete   Reply ▼   Forward ▼   Spam   Move... ▼

From:	"Luke Poole" <luke@topstuffpromotions.com>
Subject:	Re: Top Leafleter
Date:	Thu, 13 Jul 2006 16:18:28 +0100
To:	"raymond delauney" <raymonddelauney@yahoo.co.uk>

Hi Raymond,

May I have a contact number please.

Kind regards

Luke Poole
Top Stuff Promotions Limited

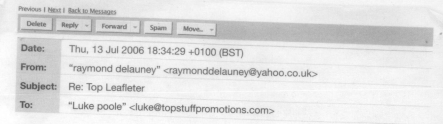

Delete | Reply ▾ | Forward ▾ | Spam | Move... ▾

Date:	Thu, 13 Jul 2006 18:34:29 +0100 (BST)
From:	"raymond delauney" <raymonddelauney@yahoo.co.uk>
Subject:	Re: Top Leafleter
To:	"Luke poole" <luke@topstuffpromotions.com>

Bloody hell!

You are clueless Poole.

I said clearly in my original mail that my mobile is out of commission and asked for you to send me your number.

I've made three trips to an internet cafe and shelled out £1.50 to get absolutely nowhere.

I've probably got a job with Sky in a call centre so you can stick your silly leafleting job, I used to dump them whenever I got the opportunity anyway.

Ray

Delete | Reply ▾ | Forward ▾ | Spam | Move... ▾

From:	"Luke Poole" <luke@topstuffpromotions.com>
Subject:	Re: Top Leafleter
Date:	Thu, 13 Jul 2006 19:07:47 +0100
To:	"raymond delauney" <raymonddelauney@yahoo.co.uk>

Raymond,

First, an apology. Sorry for not reading through your emails completely.

I tend to get more emails than I've time to read or the inclination to do so.

I've a tendency to read the first line and skim through the rest.

Otherwise, I'd have to spend a good few hours reading them.

May I suggest in future writing the below email in this succinct manner.

Lukey,

Thanks for getting back to me.

I would have replied sooner, but I'm having difficulties gaining internet access.

I've had my mobile stolen so would appreciate a contact number from you so I may call.

Are the positions available offering in advance of £4 per hour?

Are there additional benefits like complementary food?

Please be advised, I am not available every second Friday from 11 am.

I'm also available for junior office work.

Yours sincerely,

Raymond Delauney.

I can skim through this very quickly and pick up all the relevant points. Also, with regards to myself not supplying a number, if you look at the end of all my correspondence, you will note a "signature" which displays my phone number.

If things don't work out with Sky, please get in touch, as you're always welcome.

As for "clueless Poole" that made me chuckle, as yes I bloody am most of the time.

Anyway, take care and good luck Raymond.

Yours sincerely,

Luke Poole
Top Stuff Promotions Limited

END OF CORRESPONDENCE

LA PETITE ANGLAISE

Catherine Sanderson's online writings, in a blog under the name of La Petite Anglaise, brought her international attention. She has gone from out-of-work secretary to published author.

There have even been talks with film producers about the story of how her musings on life as an expat in Paris became an internet sensation…

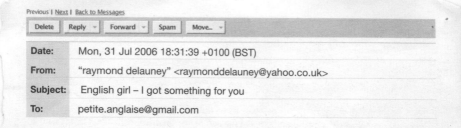

Previous | Next | Back to Messages

| Delete | Reply ▾ | Forward ▾ | Spam | Move… ▾ |

Date:	Mon, 31 Jul 2006 18:31:39 +0100 (BST)
From:	"raymond delauney" <raymonddelauney@yahoo.co.uk>
Subject:	English girl – I got something for you
To:	petite.anglaise@gmail.com

Listen Kid,

I'm a businessman. I got a 'rep' for being a straight talker.

I don't beat around the bush.

First a few blunt facts:

You've enjoyed a bit of notoriety recently. It'll wear off.

You got no chance of winning any court case – DON'T plough any dough into it.
You write well enough to get people interested in you – that's a real bonus.

Don't take this the wrong way but I find your stuff pure garbage – don't let that worry you though, I'm not essentially your audience, you've tapped into something here, no mistake.
I can make you money – I'm at the top of my game (which is PR).

I'll get you a book deal, sunshine, but I'll need a slice of the pie.

You're a good-looking cookie and pretty smart too. I've seen your type before. I know exactly how to handle artistic types.

Get back to me ASAP and don't SIGN anything.

Regards,

Raymond

| Delete | Reply ~ | Forward ~ | Spam | Move... ~ |

Date:	Mon, 31 Jul 2006 18:37:41 +0100
From:	"Petite Anglaise" <petite.anglaise@gmail.com>
To:	"raymond delauney" <raymonddelauney@yahoo.co.uk>
Subject:	Re: English girl – I got something for you

I have all the best literary agents in the UK and several publishers interested, but thank you for your email.

C

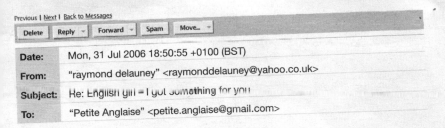

| Delete | Reply ~ | Forward ~ | Spam | Move... ~ |

Date:	Mon, 31 Jul 2006 18:50:55 +0100 (BST)
From:	"raymond delauney" <raymonddelauney@yahoo.co.uk>
Subject:	Re: English girl – I got something for you
To:	"Petite Anglaise" <petite.anglaise@gmail.com>

Hey Kid,

So you got all the 'best literary agents in the UK interested'.

Geez, didn't take long for fame to turn your head, pretty though it is.

Listen kid, I seen fame do things to people you wouldn't imagine and I'd hate to see it happen to you. Well, it wouldn't bother me too much in truth.

I've been divorced twice. One girlfriend I managed to secure a £200,000 kiss-and-tell deal. The bloody tramp kissed me goodbye as soon as the cheque cleared – without paying me my cut. I couldn't even sue her because she fled to somewhere in Switzerland. At least I slept with her though – she was a top looking broad at the time.

I know all the literary agents, I know the publishers better. They deal with me and I play hard ball with them. We gotta act soon because you won't be flavour of the month forever.

We gotta strike while the iron is hot.

I got contacts in Hollywood too, that's where the big bucks are.

Could you write something about a sailor who falls in love with a secretary who is bisexual? This would corner all the right markets.

Don't write me off kid, it'd be an expensive mistake.

Raymond

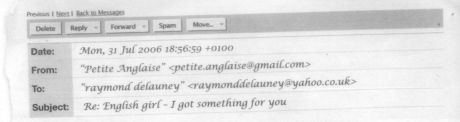

Date: Mon, 31 Jul 2006 18:56:59 +0100

From: "Petite Anglaise" <petite.anglaise@gmail.com>

To: "raymond delauney" <raymonddelauney@yahoo.co.uk>

Subject: Re: English girl – I got something for you

I think you are a fraud, or having a joke at my expense, but keep it up, my sides are splitting.

Date: Mon, 31 Jul 2006 19:06:59 +0100 (BST)

From: "raymond delauney" <raymonddelauney@yahoo.co.uk>

Subject: Re: English girl – I got something for you

To: "Petite Anglaise" <petite.anglaise@gmail.com>

FRAUD???

I have capitalised the word to indicate my raging anger.

Listen kid, I got a dinner date tonight so I'll have to insult you at greater length tomorrow.

Incidentally I want my name kept out of your blog. I treasure my privacy and I got all the work I can handle at the moment.

Just swill the contents of my mail around the back of your bonce for a bit – sleep on things. Let me know what you think when you're being a little less patronising.

Have a further think on the sailor stuff too, I am DEADLY serious. Women love men in uniform, think Richard Gere.

We'd need some love rival – I'm thinking of a woman who falls in love with a woman and a man but in the end plumps for the meat and two veg. You'll have to inject the romance angle, I ain't no good at that.

Speak later,

Raymond

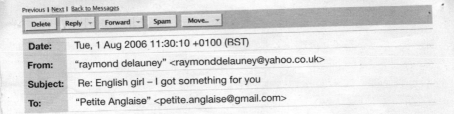

Date:	Tue, 1 Aug 2006 11:30:10 +0100 (BST)
From:	"raymond delauney" <raymonddelauney@yahoo.co.uk>
Subject:	Re: English girl – I got something for you
To:	"Petite Anglaise" <petite.anglaise@gmail.com>

Hey Kid,

I trust you've had time to think things over.

I'm out of Newark originally so you'll have to forgive my direct line of inquiry.

I realise you're getting swamped with a whole load of media attention right now but that ain't gonna last. So you need to bury the whole 'artiste' act double quick and get down to some serious thinking.

The decisions you make could have a major bearing on the next few years so it's important you make the right judgement calls.

If you jump into bed with me (speaking in business terms only) I ain't ever going to let you down.

I was instrumental in bringing Bill Oddie's book (How to Watch Wildlife) to the shelves. Bill was a massive star in the 70s.

My dinner date didn't go good last night. Fifth date, and we're still at the cheek peck stage. What's worse is when the check arrives she makes no effort to even offer to take care of it. She jabbers on about Tony Blair all night long.

Have a little think about a screenplay.

What do you think of this:

Sailor goes AWOL from serving in Iraq, falls in love with an Iraq girl. If their love is discovered she's dead meat. So he smuggles her out of the country but now he's got to dodge the UN, US and Iraqis. They almost make it but he steps on a mine near the end of the movie in Afghanistan and loses a leg. He ends up in a cell and she gets deported back to Iraq to face certain death.

It's a real tear jerker.

Raymond

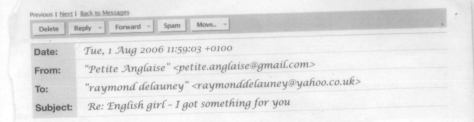

Delete | Reply ▾ | Forward ▾ | Spam | Move... ▾

Date:	*Tue, 1 Aug 2006 11:59:03 +0100*
From:	*"Petite Anglaise" <petite.anglaise@gmail.com>*
To:	*"raymond delauney" <raymonddelauney@yahoo.co.uk>*
Subject:	*Re: English girl – I got something for you*

This is too good not to publish, I'm warning you.

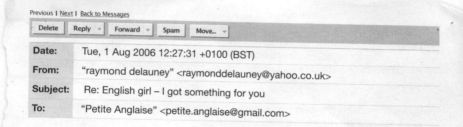

Delete | Reply ▾ | Forward ▾ | Spam | Move... ▾

Date:	Tue, 1 Aug 2006 12:27:31 +0100 (BST)
From:	"raymond delauney" <raymonddelauney@yahoo.co.uk>
Subject:	Re: English girl – I got something for you
To:	"Petite Anglaise" <petite.anglaise@gmail.com>

Cmon Kid,

I'm throwing you a lifeline here – and you issue me a warning?

Don't seem like a fair deal to me.

I think you and I could corroborate successfully on a globally impacting project.

You got the chick flick angle covered whilst I can cater for the way the man's brain interprets cinematic imagery and plot.

I'd rather you didn't replicate my kind hearted offer of help on your blog (we need to navigate away from this area) but if you feel you have to mention my name then please spell it correctly.

Raymond

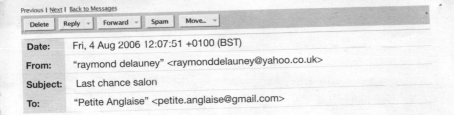

Date:	Fri, 4 Aug 2006 12:07:51 +0100 (BST)
From:	"raymond delauney" <raymonddelauney@yahoo.co.uk>
Subject:	Last chance salon
To:	"Petite Anglaise" <petite.anglaise@gmail.com>

Hey Big Cheese,

Last chance salon.

I always thought that'd make a good name for a hairdressers.

I'll keep this Oxford dictionary concise because, for whatever reason, you ain't getting any of my serves back. And it's annoying me.

I don't care who it is I work with – whether it be a nobody or a Bill Oddie – I demand some level of common courtesy.

All I'm trying to do is help you across unfamiliar terrain, shine a torch, shed some light on an industry that's covered in crap. OK, so I'll skim a little cream off the top of I can, that's par for the course.

Right now I guess the corporate boys are rolling out the red carpet, sucking on cappuccinos and filling your head with figures plucked from the ozone layer.

Let me tell you a little bit about me:

I swim with sharks every day of the week. I can trade bullshit with the best of 'em, I've pitched to all the big hitters and I've heard all the buzz words.

I can get you guaranteed numbers.

I'm a down the middle guy. I call things how I see 'em.

I'm good, I'm very good.

Hollywood is where the honey is. If we can hit on something original it could be me and you quay side in Monaco sipping a cold one watching the swanky yachts sail on by.

Have a think about things kid...

Raymond

| Delete | Reply ▾ | Forward ▾ | Spam | Move... ▾ |

Date:	Fri, 11 Aug 2006 11:42:26 +0100 (BST)
From:	"raymond delauney" <raymonddelauney@yahoo.co.uk>
Subject:	POSSIBLE DEAL
To:	"Petite Anglaise" <petite.anglaise@gmail.com>

Hey Kid,

Apologies – I've been very busy on the other projects and accordingly had to put your Bunsen on the back burner for now.

On a side issue I have sent a couple of scripts over to a few producer friends – I've not had any initial feedback yet which is a good sign as we've not been rejected out of hand. I suspect they may contact me with an offer on the sailor film (Bowled Over in Basra).

I've mentioned you'd like to be on board once I've finalised a few figures. How old are you? Might be able to help you out with an advertising deal.

I got a couple of marketing contacts who are keen to push **pentapeptides.** It's some bullshit cream that makes the skin look younger. Undoubtedly a bag of crap but the guys at oil of Ulay did okay out of something similar. What do you reckon a ulay is, anyway?

They've slapped a scientific name on it with a fancy price and expect it to shift off the shelves – bought by gullible broads (that's all of them, then). Someone told me I was gullible once – and I believed him!

I might be able to cut a sponsorship deal. How many hits does your site get? In that blog of yours you say something along the lines of:

"Woke up today, feeling groggy after an interminable night of tossing and turning, my satin nighty chafing my thighs etc

I tried some pentapeptides last night (from Boots at £12.99) and I was amazed at how much younger my skin looks. "

Have a think on it,

Raymond

END OF CORRESPONDENCE
(but much discussed on La Petite Anglaise blog)

DIARY OF A SWORDSMAN

Date:	Thu, 19 Jan 2006 16:43:03 +0000 (GMT)
From:	"raymond delauney" <raymonddelauney@yahoo.co.uk>
Subject:	Hi Emma
To:	emma@sodamagazine.co.uk

Hi Emma,

My publicist informed me over lunch of your magazine's impending launch. I dined on a light pasta con Funghi at Carluccios in Covent Garden. If the little Italian gets one thing consistently right it's his Funghi. Absolutely sumptuous.

I'd like to proffer my insincere congratulations on securing the editorship of 'Soda'. I wouldn't dream of patronising you by suggesting your publication will be a runaway triumph. I have no ideas as to your abilities and consequently would be ill placed to form an accurate assessment of your project's chances of success or failure. I should imagine it'll probably end in tears. I am however prepared to bid you the very best of British luck.

As you are doubtless aware your publication couldn't be competing in a more crowded marketplace. Editorially I may suggest that you offer something dissimilar from the dulling crowd. Perhaps a feature on the middle-aged Turkish woman who marries a young English waiter.

I'm sure you have deadlines to miss so I'll keep this as brief as possible and trust that you are conscientious or curious enough to skim over what could prove to be the 'whisky' to your soda. I personally favour bitter lemon as a mixer. Nevertheless, I suppose one could hardly expect you to name your magazine, Bitter Lemon.

If your magazines are going to shift from the sardine packed shelves you and your scribes really need to be writing about the very things women are interested in. This leads me rather neatly to my next point.

What are women really interested in?

You can categorise women according to age, income or breast size (I'm more of a log man, myself). But, you take it from me, an authority on the fairer sex, ladies are interested in precisely the same two subjects as their male counterparts, namely – sex and success. I embody both qualities.

I say 'sex', but what I really mean is sex dressed up, dusted down and packaged as 'romance'. The difference is subtle with Hollywood knowing precisely where, what, who and how to package it. The 'who' is invariably played by that dithering dunce Hugh Grant. To be fair to him, he does it well.

So now you're probably wondering who the hell I am and what I want. People like me generally want something.

Who is Raymond Delauney?

I would immodestly describe myself as the kind of guy your readers will be fascinated by. The type of man your readers dream about dating.

I guess the tabloid term for a guy like me is a 'gigolo'. I detest this particular description with every ounce of my intellectual might. It suggests someone like me simply exploits women for monetary gain. Whilst this interpretation is not entirely inaccurate I consider myself an average great looking guy with the rare ability to respond and react to women's dreams and desires. A quality like this is exceptional thus highly sought after and therefore expensive. I'm also very good in the sack.

I've bedded somewhere in the region of 2,000 women. At first I did it because I could. Later, I utilised this sexual gift as a way to secure my future. Ever since I've been old enough to work – I haven't. This is without doubt my greatest achievement.

Very few women ever split with me on bad terms. Out of the 2,000 I've been in I'd say only 200 or so felt ill of me. This may sound a lot but on closer analysis that figure is actually under 10%. I include my first wife here, who I stupidly married for love.

I am merely a charming guy from the lower orders of the aristocracy. In total I have had three wives. I am 56 – but only look around 52.

I suggest you write about me as a case study. I am not after fiscal reward so much as exposure for my soon-to-launch book autobiography,

Isn't He Delovely by Raymond Delauney.

The Story of a Swordsman

Will Include:

- My steamy affair with Anthea Redfern (Generation Game)
- How I tracked down and became a father to my 17 kids
- The story of drugs, scandal and an actress from Triangle (old soap)
- My orgy with a famous rock band (The Flying Pickets)
- The hooker who broke my heart

My publicist also suggested the possibility of the following competition:

Your readers could win a Date with Delauney.

The winner would pay for the meal and if we got along the lady in question could come back to my hotel room – if they are good looking enough and I feel the conditions are right I may sleep with her. I am single and there would be no charge on this occasion as long as I get a good write up about the book.

If you would like to meet with me over dinner to discuss this further please reply.

Raymond Delauney

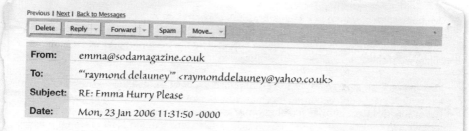

Delete	Reply ▾	Forward ▾	Spam	Move... ▾

From:	emma@sodamagazine.co.uk
To:	"'raymond delauney'" <raymonddelauney@yahoo.co.uk>
Subject:	RE: Emma Hurry Please
Date:	Mon, 23 Jan 2006 11:31:50 -0000

Raymond!

Thank you for your delightful email. Unfortunately at this point I am unable to consider your proposal, although from the sounds of it this could lead to a nation of disappointed women.
As much as I would love to be taken out to dinner by yourself, I'm afraid my schedule is too busy to allow it. I may live to regret this decision but must take the chance on this occasion.
I wish you all the best and hope to see you gracing the pages of a magazine very soon.
Best wishes,
Emma

Editor

Date:	Tue, 24 Jan 2006 14:53:26 +0000 (GMT)
From:	"raymond delauney" <raymonddelauney@yahoo.co.uk>
Subject:	UPDATE
To:	emma@sodamagazine.co.uk

Hi Emma,

It's me again, Raymond Delauney.

Just to keep you in the loop I feel I should let you know that the Deputy Editor of Golden Oldies magazine is practically salivating at the mere prospect of meeting me. We will discuss a possible collaboration.

I believe she's a single mother. I've suggested we meet for a Spanish omelette.

I'm sure Golden Oldies' readership would be captivated by a man like myself. I'd like to commit to a deal although I hold reservations that the subject matter might be a little too saucy for their taste.

Even though I'm 56 I look and act a lot younger. I can still get away with wearing a pair of leather trousers, for example.

My only concern is that your readers might be missing out to the middle-aged slipper shufflers. I think your readership is a better 'fit' – racy housewives who still like a bit of slap and tickle and have probably flattened a bit of grass in their time.

Who shall I deal with – you or Golden Oldies?

I'm still open to offers.

I could put the fizz in your magazine if given the chance.

Raymond

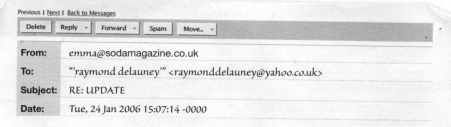

Delete | Reply ▾ | Forward ▾ | Spam | Move… ▾

From:	emma@sodamagazine.co.uk
To:	"'raymond delauney'" <raymonddelauney@yahoo.co.uk>
Subject:	RE: UPDATE
Date:	Tue, 24 Jan 2006 15:07:14 -0000

Dear Raymond,

Thank you for your kind email informing me of your possible future feature with Golden Oldies magazine. I certainly imagine that if this goes ahead the readers will be delighted and enthralled by your contribution.

As for your concern over the 'middle aged slipper shufflers', I think you may be surprised by the reception your racy subject matter will get. My grandmother is 76 and can regularly be found out and about in her gold leather trousers with matching handbag.

Best of luck,

Emma

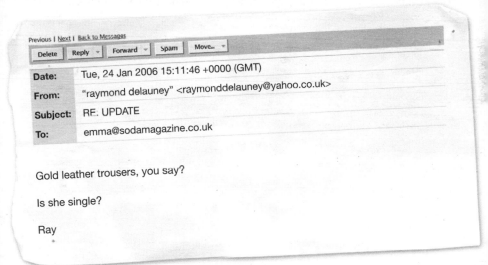

Delete | Reply ▾ | Forward ▾ | Spam | Move… ▾

Date:	Tue, 24 Jan 2006 15:11:46 +0000 (GMT)
From:	"raymond delauney" <raymonddelauney@yahoo.co.uk>
Subject:	RE: UPDATE
To:	emma@sodamagazine.co.uk

Gold leather trousers, you say?

Is she single?

Ray

NO REPLY

127

SAME MAIL SENT TO EDITOR OF GOLDEN OLDIES MAGAZINE

Delete	Reply ˅	Forward ˅	Spam	Move... ˅

To:	raymonddelauney@yahoo.co.uk
Subject:	Many thanks
From:	michelle.todd@goldenoldies.co.uk
Date:	Mon, 23 Jan 2006 15:49:49 +0000

Thanks for your amusing email. Not the School for Scoundrel Raymond, by any chance?

Your story is something that sounds very intriguing, but perhaps something better timed around the launch of your autobiography. Do let me know the name of the publisher and publicist and I will be sure to stay on the ball, as far as that is concerned.

Thank you for thinking of us.

Michelle Todd
Deputy Editor, Golden Oldie Magazine

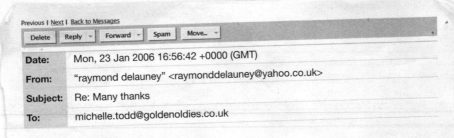

Delete	Reply ˅	Forward ˅	Spam	Move... ˅

Date:	Mon, 23 Jan 2006 16:56:42 +0000 (GMT)
From:	"raymond delauney" <raymonddelauney@yahoo.co.uk>
Subject:	Re: Many thanks
To:	michelle.todd@goldenoldies.co.uk

Dearest Michelle,

Funny you should mention I share the same name as the School for Scoundrels character, very few people remember this classic film.

I'm terribly encouraged you replied.

What you must remember, Michelle, is that a lifetime of mixing with minxes has left me well placed to unravel the complex inner workings of the female psyche.

I noted in your response that you tellingly signed off with your name and full address at the bottom of the mail. Cheeky! I would suggest this is not the course of action one would necessarily perform if one didn't hope to hear from me again. Michelle, my dear, if you wish for the mountain to make its way to Mohammed you should simply have mentioned it in the first place. As experienced and expert as I am in dealing with the fairer sex you lot can be jolly frustrating at times.

If you would care to buy me lunch I would readily agree. I feel strongly drawn towards marinated scallops with a light truffle salad for some reason.

I'm not easily beaten off with a stick – or any other object for that matter. One irate husband, having disturbed me mid climax with his highly sexed wife, started hacking through the bolted bedroom door with an axe, forcing me to make an urgent exit via a first floor window. In modern parlance I was playing the over paid Chelsea showboater, Joe Cole to Jack Nicholson's portrayal of abusive husband, Jack Torrance in The Shining. Like Joe, I got the hell out of there, fast.

I took flight barefoot and completely naked through a busy Clapham High Street for what seemed an eternity, but was probably only 12 minutes. I caused much consternation and considerable amusement among passer-by's and pedestrians alike until a kindly road sweeper came to my rescue by allowing me to borrow his spare pair of waterproof bottoms, which lay underneath a compressed tuna sandwich in his dustcart.

The grimy outfit looked as though it hadn't seen the inside of a washing machine for an awfully long time, possibly years. It was without doubt the filthiest, smelliest and most ill fitting garment that I have ever been so overjoyed to wear.

When a sharp blade is being swung toward you with considerable force and the distinct likelihood it may nestle in the base of your skull, trying to locate the exact whereabouts of one's pantaloons is very much a low priority. I hope you never have to find that out.

The full details relating to this story can be found in Chapter 7 of my book.

I should mention that, like a cunning poker player, I didn't declare my entire hand in my earlier email. I failed to allude to the juicer, chunky chapters of my book, preferring instead to save these delights for the forthcoming unveiling of 'Isn't He Delovely' (by Raymond Delauney).

I will however reveal that two of my more famous liaisons include the delightful Lorraine Chase and the less likeable Shirley Bassey, who issued a restraining order against me.

I can also supply priceless information on what men look for in women, although this is no great mystery – a pretty face and a pert pair of headlamps tends to do the trick for me!

I have perfected a massage technique that results in a 95% sex conversion rate once applied to a woman – if I could market this I'd be a millionaire overnight. Do you think a Men's magazine would pay handsomely for it?

Discreetly Delauney

I could be tempted to model some swimwear or be photographed hiding my modesty with, say, a bunch of grapes, should your readers demand it. I work out regularly and I'm still in pretty good shape for my age. I'd require remuneration of sorts for this – along with web rights, if applicable.

I think it would be better to strike now before the inevitable furore the book launch will cause. The News of the World are in talks for serialisation rights.

Be brave and commission my piece, Michelle.

The ball appears to be very much on your side of the net.

Best regards,

Raymond Delauney

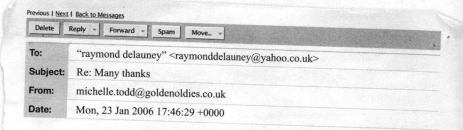

Previous I Next I Back to Messages

| Delete | Reply ▾ | Forward ▾ | Spam | Move... ▾ |

To:	"raymond delauney" <raymonddelauney@yahoo.co.uk>
Subject:	Re: Many thanks
From:	michelle.todd@goldenoldies.co.uk
Date:	Mon, 23 Jan 2006 17:46:29 +0000

And the publisher is?

Michelle Todd
Deputy Editor, Golden Oldie Magazine

END OF CORRESPONDENCE

SAME MAIL TO FARRAH HALL, EDITOR OF NEWSTYLE MAGAZINE

| Delete | Reply ▾ | Forward ▾ | Spam | Move... ▾ |

Subject:	RE: Hi Farrah – force this to be commissioned!
Date:	Wed, 25 Jan 2006 11:46:32 -0000
From:	"Farrah Hall" <Farrah.hall@newstylemag.co.uk>
To:	"raymond delauney" <raymonddelauney@yahoo.co.uk>

Hi Raymond,

Is this a joke? If not, I'm really flattered that you thought of us with your amazing story.

However, as you're probably aware our magazine is aimed at the 20–30 market so I don't think your story would be quite right. I honestly don't think they would relate to the marriages, 17 kids etc. as well as an older audience.

However, I am more than happy to have a chat with some of my other journalist friends. To be totally honest I'm not sure which women's mag would run your story, as women's mags (and I've worked for everyone from HouseSmart to Caring to Today's Women) are notorious for only going to women's stories.

However I do have friends at men's magazines ShowOff! and Bloke and although I know they're not your ideal target I think they would be more interested from a human interest angle.

If you are happy for me to speak with them then please let me know.

Good Luck

Farrah

131

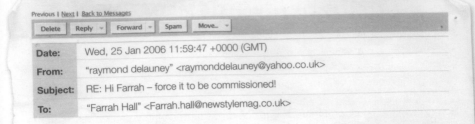

| Delete | Reply ▾ | Forward ▾ | Spam | Move... ▾ |

Date:	Wed, 25 Jan 2006 11:59:47 +0000 (GMT)
From:	"raymond delauney" <raymonddelauney@yahoo.co.uk>
Subject:	RE: Hi Farrah – force it to be commissioned!
To:	"Farrah Hall" <Farrah.hall@newstylemag.co.uk>

Hi Farrah,

Yes the joke was 'Farrah (force-it) to be commissioned.' I don't know if you are too young to remember but there was a famous actress by the name of Farrah Fawcett who acted in the 1970s – she was an original Charlie's Angel, only second in looks to the lovely Jacklyn Smith. I bought the Playboy mag when she (Farrah) stripped in it and wasn't disappointed – great body.

| Delete | Reply ▾ | Forward ▾ | Spam | Move... ▾ |

Subject:	RE: Hi Farrah – force it to be commissioned!
Date:	Wed, 25 Jan 2006 12:05:07 -0000
From:	"Farrah Hall" <Farrah.hall@newstylemag.co.uk>
To:	"raymond delauney" <raymonddelauney@yahoo.co.uk>

I will see if they are interested.

Thanks

Subject:	RE: Hi Farrah – force it to be commissioned!
Date:	Wed, 25 Jan 2006 12:08:10 -0000
From:	"Farrah Hall" <Farrah.hall@newstylemag.co.uk>
To:	"raymond delauney" <raymonddelauney@yahoo.co.uk>

Sorry Raymond – just one more thing. Could you tell me who your publicist is?

Many thanks

Date:	Wed, 25 Jan 2006 12:12:12 +0000 (GMT)
From:	"raymond delauney" <raymonddelauney@yahoo.co.uk>
Subject:	RE: Hi Farrah – force it to be commissioned!
To:	"Farrah Hall" <Farrah.hall@newstylemag.co.uk>

Thanks Farrah,

My publicist is an ex-girlfriend who I still get on great with – she's called Roberta Thornley-Jenkins.

Best regards,

Raymond

Subject:	RE: Hi Farrah – force it to be commissioned!
Date:	Wed, 25 Jan 2006 12:31:41 -0000
From:	"Farrah Hall" <Farrah.hall@newstylemag.co.uk>
To:	"raymond delauney" <raymonddelauney@yahoo.co.uk>

One last thing – do you know how she knew about my new position at NewStyle?

Date:	Wed, 25 Jan 2006 15:16:17 +0000 (GMT)
From:	"raymond delauney" <raymonddelauney@yahoo.co.uk>
Subject:	RE: Hi Farrah – force it to be commissioned!
To:	"Farrah Hall" <Farrah.hall@newstylemag.co.uk>

Farrah,

Did you get the Farrah Force It joke? Farrah Fawcett later married Ryan O'Neal – I'm surprised you've never heard of her.

Roberta is a damn good PR girl. She has lists of all the important people in Town, obviously you are among them. You must be doing something right.

I dare say you'll be head hunted at some time with that impressive CV of yours.

Do you know the editor of Soda? Bloody rude woman.

Best regards,

Raymond

Subject:	RE: Hi Farrah – force it to be commissioned!
Date:	Thu, 26 Jan 2006 10:42:33 -0000
From:	"Farrah Hall" <Farrah.hall@newstylemag.co.uk>
To:	"raymond delauney" <raymonddelauney@yahoo.co.uk>

Hi Raymond,

I had a word with my friend at ShowOff! -and he seems quite interested. I'm going to forward him your email this morning – but do you have a picture as well that you could email over?

Many thanks

Date:	Tue, 31 Jan 2006 08:48:20 +0000 (GMT)
From:	"raymond delauney" <raymonddelauney@yahoo.co.uk>
Subject:	RE: Hi Farrah – force it to be commissioned!
To:	"Farrah Hall" <Farrah.hall@newstylemag.co.uk>

Hi Farrah,

A thousand apologies for not responding to your mail of last week and many thanks for being kind enough to tap your contact at ShowOff! on my behalf. I dare say he'll be deeply indebted to us once we've been responsible for widening their circulation.

Is there a chance I might feature on the front cover? I've not heard of the magazine before – is it anything to do with Melvyn Bragg?

I may take you for a meal by way of a thank you should the whole show draw out to the amicable conclusion I anticipate. Do you care for spinach ricotta?

I have just journeyed back from Stockholm where I stayed at an old flame's place. She is the mother to one of my sons, Henrik. I must say the little devil does remind me of the way I looked and acted when I was around his age – except he speaks Swedish! It's funny how all the kids have their own little personalities. I know it's wrong to have favourites but this chap is a real smasher and I try and pop back every birthday to check on his progress.

If he has inherited his father's roving eye and overactive libido he's growing up in the right place. Scandinavian women are, in my humble opinion, among the best looking sorts in the world, with the Norwegian brigade the most adventurous in the bedroom. I have a theory that when the Vikings conquered Scotland they returned home with only the good looking ones – this would go some way to explaining the shabby state of the women north of Hadrian's wall and the high proportion of redheads. Sorry if you are Scottish – or a redhead. I love red hair on women however my experiences with ginger men (husbands) have led me to conclude them to be quick tempered and violent.

I must confess to being glad to head home when I did, the rigours of parenthood tend to have an exhausting, ageing effect.

May I suggest that if your fellows from ShowOff! are amenable I could send them an all-encompassing article detailing my extraordinary life. I think you chaps would refer to it as an 'exclusive'. I won't require a fee however a small cheque to a charity of my choice would be appreciated. How many words would they want?

I have personally written every word of **Isn't He Delovely by Raymond Delaney, the Story of a Swordsman** (the title was also my idea). I may have a cemetery full of skeletons in my cupboard but absolutely no ghosts!

I can supply photos as well as an all encompassing article. And don't worry Farrah, I'll send it to you and the girls at your mag to quench your fervent curiosity.

I shall include advice on the following:

How to get a woman into bed
My massage technique that makes women demand sex
How to end a relationship on good terms
Narrow escapes from irate husbands
Tips on making women spend money on you
What women really want to hear

All the best,

Raymond

Delete   Reply ▾   Forward ▾   Spam   Move... ▾

Subject:	RE: Hi Farrah – force it to be commissioned!
Date:	Fri, 3 Feb 2006 10:59:22 -0000
From:	"Farrah Hall" <Farrah.hall@newstylemag.co.uk>
To:	"raymond delauney" <raymonddelauney@yahoo.co.uk>

Sorry Raymond,

I don't know what's happening with ShowOff! My partner is the contact there and I have passed on your details. He is off for the next week, but should be in touch shortly if they plan on doing anything with you.

Best of luck with everything and I look forward to seeing the book at a Waterstones soon.

F

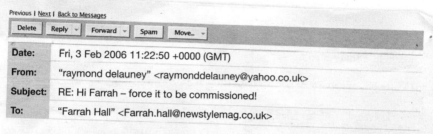

Previous | Next | Back to Messages

| Delete | Reply ▾ | Forward ▾ | Spam | Move... ▾ |

Date:	Fri, 3 Feb 2006 11:22:50 +0000 (GMT)
From:	"raymond delauney" <raymonddelauney@yahoo.co.uk>
Subject:	RE: Hi Farrah – force it to be commissioned!
To:	"Farrah Hall" <Farrah.hall@newstylemag.co.uk>

Sorry, Farrah, to hear you have a partner that is!

Regardless of whether ShowOff! decide to enter the arena of Raymond G. Delauney you shall have a signed copy sent to you along with a photo of how I looked in my prime – I am wearing leather trousers but do not look camp. I cut a dashing figure in those days.

All the very best of luck,

Raymond

END OF CORRESPONDENCE

EXTREME SPORTS

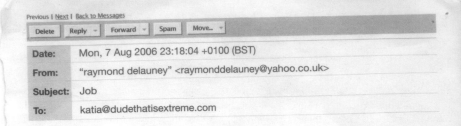

Delete	Reply ▾ Forward ▾ Spam Move... ▾

Date:	Mon, 7 Aug 2006 23:18:04 +0100 (BST)
From:	"raymond delauney" <raymonddelauney@yahoo.co.uk>
Subject:	Job
To:	katia@dudethatisextreme.com

Hi,

I want to work with you guys.

Put simply, extreme sports is my life.

My professional background is in sports journalism. I know pretty much everything about skiing, slalom and bobsleighing. I enjoy white water rafting and occasionally some black water rafting when the weather allows, but my passion is extreme sports. The more extreme the better.

I'd be ideally suited to heading up your web content division. I can bring sponsorship to the party should I be handed the right package. Red Bull throw money at me all the time. I'm flexible.

I don't really deal in CVs but if you want to have a chat or perhaps meet up and say throw ourselves out of a plane together, then I'd certainly be up for that.

Who Is Raymond Delauney?

Someone who lives life to the full. I'm pretty sociable although in truth I have few real friends in life, partly because I prefer to push myself, and others, to the limit. I lost my one real pal, Kevin Harper-Harper during a sky dive in 2002 that went fatally wrong. I still have it on video cam.

I get my kicks from risking my life and living life to the full. Double H felt the same way as me. LIVE life or die trying.

My chief interests are kite surfing, hang gliding, barefoot water skiing and a bit of street luge when I get the time. I also enjoy a good game of bowls.

I used to enjoy roller blading too until a nasty accident caused me to dislocate my knee for a second time, worse still, it kept me inactive for a while. Ironic really, I never had any problems throwing myself out of planes for 8 years and yet an uncoordinated four-year-old rushes unavoidably into my path and puts me on crutches!

The kid was fine save for the fact she lost both her front teeth (one was actually embedded in my knee pad). Astonishingly her money mad parents actually attempted to sue me. It's not as if I knocked her teeth out on purpose. It was only her first set of teeth anyway, as I told them, I only wish I could grow back my old knee.

Compensation culture gone mad.

I enjoy taking sport to a different dimension and so an element of risk is a necessary, in fact essential ingredient, in any pursuit I partake in. I look for the same quality in a job and this is why I gave up accountancy. I think you guys would understand that more than most.

Let me know your gut reaction and if I'm the type of guy you think you could use.

Raymond

Previous | Next | Back to Messages

| Delete | Reply ▾ | Forward ▾ | Spam | Move... ▾ |

To:	"raymond delauney" <raymonddelauney@yahoo.co.uk>
Subject:	FROM KATIA AT THE EXTREME GROUP
From:	katia@dudethatisextreme.com
Date:	Wed, 9 Aug 2006 12:01:56 +0100

Dear Raymond

Thank you for your letter. Unfortunately we are not recruiting in this field at present. However, your background seems quite unique, so I will keep you in mind for any future vacancies.

We are at the very early research and development stages on a few large-scale projects, so please keep updated via our website.

Kind regards

Katia

Assistant
& Special Projects Manager
Dude That Is Extreme Group

END OF CORRESPONDENCE

JAN LEEMING

Delete | Reply ▾ | Forward ▾ | Spam | Move... ▾

Date:	Sun, 12 Nov 2006 15:16:53 +0000 (GMT)
From:	"raymond delauney" <raymonddelauney@yahoo.co.uk>
Subject:	Jan Leeming scoop
To:	scoops@sundaycorrespondent.co.uk

Hi,

In your newspaper you ask for stories relating to any of the 'celebrities' appearing on 'I'm a celebrity get me out of here!'

I used to live next to Jan Leeming and I can tell you something about her that will make you see her in an absolutely different light to the posh newsreader the public perceive her to be.

I have photos.

Raymond

Delete | Reply ▾ | Forward ▾ | Spam | Move... ▾

Subject:	from Tristan
To:	raymonddelauney@yahoo.co.uk
From:	Tristan.fido@sundaycorrespondent.co.uk
Date:	Tue, 14 Nov 2006 10:48:46 +0000

Sir,

My name is Tristan Fido, I am a reporter at the Sunday Correspondent newspaper. Your email has been passed on to me by the newsdesk. It is the most intriguing email I have ever read! It would be absolutely brilliant to speak to you about Jan Leeming.

Of course, if you wish you can remain totally anonymous if eventually any story is published.

We could also meet you and give you a "confidentiality agreement" meaning we couldn't publish anything you told us without your consent.

Please contact me as soon as you possibly can on 07951 576071, and I'll call you straight back to save the phone bill.

Many thanks again.

Tristan

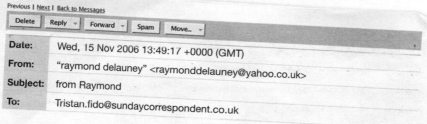

| Delete | Reply ˅ | Forward ˅ | Spam | Move... ˅ |

Date:	Wed, 15 Nov 2006 13:49:17 +0000 (GMT)
From:	"raymond delauney" <raymonddelauney@yahoo.co.uk>
Subject:	from Raymond
To:	Tristan.fido@sundaycorrespondent.co.uk

Sorry,

Been busy.

Will drop you a mail with the story tonight, but will need a financial injection should you decide to use the material.

I think it'll offer an interesting side to Ms Leeming that people never knew existed.

Least of all me!!

Raymond

| Delete | Reply ˅ | Forward ˅ | Spam | Move... ˅ |

Subject:	Re: from Raymond
To:	"raymond delauney" <raymonddelauney@yahoo.co.uk>
From:	Tristan.fido@sundaycorrespondent.co.uk
Date:	Wed, 15 Nov 2006 14:02:38 +0000

Hi Raymond,

Thanks for the email.

Once everything has been checked we will be happy to pay for the story, no problem.

If you are happy to do so, please include a phone number in your email so we can talk about the story – or please contact me on my mobile, 07951 576071.

Thanks again, I look forward to reading about what happened!

Tristan

Tristan,

I used to live next-door but one from Jan in the mid 1980s.

In those days she certainly fitted the bill of the classy 'older' woman. Always smartly dressed, but slightly stuck up, she looked every inch like she belonged to the high society set. Every bloke in our street fancied the pants off her. Me included.

Jan always had a smile for me whenever we chatted in the street or bumped into each other. It wasn't just me that noticed, the wife used to remark quite often that Jan fancied me. I don't mind admitting I cut a handsome figure in those days. I had a full head of hair, a brand new Volvo estate and a good job selling photocopiers. They were very easy to shift in those days.

Unfortunately, I was married (had 2 wives since), and so was Jan. If we were both single I would definitely have asked her to dine with me and I fancy she would have agreed.

Anyway, my wife and I were invited to a house party of hers. The conversation soon got round to her front lawn whereupon she asked if she could borrow my lawnmower.

In those days I had a very expensive lawn mower. The type you sit down in and drive. I readily agreed to loan her it, as well as a leaf rake and a gardening trowel. I like to help people out where I can.

Incredibly, she kept the lawnmower for three weeks without ever hinting at returning it – I actually had to knock on her door and ask for it back. Only to discover her husband had loaned it to somebody else!!! It wasn't his to loan out, was it?

I didn't get it back for another fortnight after that.

What's worse is I never saw the (leaf) rake or the trowel again. The onus was on her to hand them back, not on me to ask for my possessions back.

So she effectively stole them from me.

I just gave her the occasional nod after that – I didn't even bother stopping to talk to her.

It just goes to show how the rich and famous think they can treat 'ordinary' folk like us.

How much would this story be worth, do you think?

I still have the lawnmower in my garage. It's not functional anymore though but could be used for photographic purposes.

Regards,

Raymond

Previous | Next | Back to Messages

Delete	Reply ▾	Forward ▾	Spam	Move... ▾

Subject:	Re: from Raymond
To:	"raymond delauney" <raymonddelauney@yahoo.co.uk>
From:	Tristan.fido@sundaycorrespondent.co.uk
Date:	Thu, 16 Nov 2006 16:14:49 +0000

Hi Raymond,

Yes, there is scope for getting a few quid out of the story.

I really need to speak to you to make it happen.

I want to check several things with you.

We will also need to get a picture of you, too, if possible!

Please call me as soon as you can, 07951 576071.

You MUST do this as soon as possible so that we can progress with this story – it doesn't matter what time it is.

Thanks,

Tristan

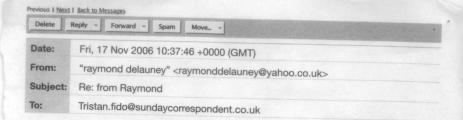

Delete | Reply ▼ | Forward ▼ | Spam | Move... ▼

Date:	Fri, 17 Nov 2006 10:37:46 +0000 (GMT)
From:	"raymond delauney" <raymonddelauney@yahoo.co.uk>
Subject:	Re: from Raymond
To:	Tristan.fido@sundaycorrespondent.co.uk

Tristan,

Thanks for your response.

I need to nail down a figure before I pick up the phone. That figure will be non-negotiable.

I live in a very posh part of Surrey and for me to have my name in the papers and the neighbours talking about me I'll need appropriate compensation.

I know you journalists have a bad reputation when it comes to straight talking. I made my money in sales.

So, we'll need to nail down a concrete contract saying you guys will pay me £5k – that price includes a photo of the Lawnflite Ride. That is a non-nego deal, as we say in sales.

Regards,

Raymond

Delete | Reply ▼ | Forward ▼ | Spam | Move... ▼

Subject:	Re: from Raymond
To:	"raymond delauney" <raymonddelauney@yahoo.co.uk>
From:	Tristan.fido@sundaycorrespondent.co.uk
Date:	Fri, 17 Nov 2006 10:55:32 +0000

Hi Raymond,

I don't think we could pay £5k, but please give me a call and we can sort something out – the story will probably be no longer than eight paragraphs so £5k is far too much! Please give me a call... 07951 576071

Tristan

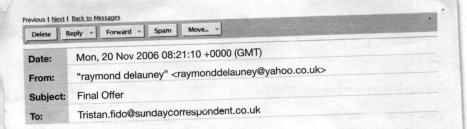

Date:	Mon, 20 Nov 2006 08:21:10 +0000 (GMT)
From:	"raymond delauney" <raymonddelauney@yahoo.co.uk>
Subject:	Final Offer
To:	Tristan.fido@sundaycorrespondent.co.uk

Tristan,

Brass tacks:

I want £5k for the lawnmower story, that's a bargain. Your readers will lap it up on a Sunday. It's precisely the kind of story they need to read.

Alternatively I'll take £10k if I say I slept with Jan.

She won't be able to prove any different unless they put me through a DNA test, which is unlikely, isn't it? If they do then I can disappear to my place in Mallorca for a while until things blow over. We could mix this in with the lawnmower story.

Both prices are non-nego. It might even affect my divorce payments so I'll need what I'm asking.

I don't negotiate downwards,

Raymond

NO REPLY

PEOPLE HELPERS

JOB AD

Hello.

We're innocent and we make 100% fresh fruit smoothies that taste good and are good for you. We were set up by three good friends, Jon, Richard and Adam. In the summer of 1998, they bought £500 worth of fruit, turned it into smoothies and took them to a jazz festival to try out their idea. They put up a big sign saying 'Do you think we should give up our jobs to make these smoothies?' and put out a bin saying 'YES' and a bin saying 'NO', asking people to try one of their drinks and then to put their empty bottle in the appropriate bin. At the end of the weekend, the 'YES' bin was full so they went to work the next day and resigned.

Now, 7 years later, we're the fastest-growing drinks company in the UK and there are 136 of us now working at innocent across the UK and continental Europe.

Can you fly? Are you really handy at organising stock and offering support to a team and managing a fleet of vans? If so, then maybe you're the one for us. We're looking for an office superhero to join us here at innocent's Fruit Towers in London.

You'll need to be energetic and enthusiastic to manage our stock and maintain our loading bay. You'll be the point of contact for all couriers, managing the relationship and service with them, so best be friendly, efficient and customer-service oriented. You will be the point of contact for our fleet of lovingly cared for cow vans; making sure that someone feeds and waters them so they are fresh as a daisy when they need to go for a run.

Being a team player is important as you will be working with a whole bunch of people and helping out in the office where necessary (this may include various handyman tasks so have your tool belt ready). You'll need to be organised and take the initiative, using your problem solving skills to deal with any queries that arise relating to stock controls, general office issues and Clarke Kent movie trivia.

In terms of qualifications, you'll have good A levels (or equivalent), as well as a clean driver's licence. Stock management and handyman experience would also be useful for changing light bulbs as is experience of dealing with people on the phone. You need to have good interpersonal skills and ability to deal with people at all levels.

Luckily, there is no requirement for you to wear your underpants on the outside of your trousers, although if you want to, you may wear a cape.

If you think you've got what it takes to be our superhero, we'd love to hear from you. Please go to our website: www.innocentdrinks.co.uk/jobs to find details on how to apply.

Please send applications by midnight on Monday 14th August.

Love from innocent X

| Delete | Reply ▾ | Forward ▾ | Spam | Move... ▾ |

Date:	Mon, 21 Aug 2006 10:19:11 +0100 (BST)
From:	"raymond delauney" <raymonddelauney@yahoo.co.uk>
Subject:	Advert on Gumtree
To:	jobs@innocentdrinks.co.uk

NOTE: SECOND TIME I'VE SENT THIS MAIL

Hello,

I've read your ad.

I don't think you needed the lengthy prologue about the bosses and the bins.

Seeing people doing worse than me generally makes me feel better, not the other way round.

Admittedly, making people part with upwards of two nuggets for a couple of mouthfuls of cordial is a feat worthy of bragging. I think it'd be better to pat each other on the back amongst yourselves rather than expect people in need of lowly paid work to flip somersaults in celebration.

I see you're advertising for an 'office superhero'. To be perfectly candid I'd suggest you don't need someone with special powers at all.

A person who is reasonably competent would meet the criteria. Somebody capable of ordering quantities of fruit on the phone. A man or woman who would be content with being paid a fraction of the profit his bosses earn and be prepared to gush at how clever they were.

I threw thirty years of life savings down the toilet by buying a half share in a restaurant venture. I'm not inviting people round to my threadbare bedsit to call me a thick twat. I know it; my ex-wife knows it and she has a very annoying habit of reminding me of it every single day.

One other thing:

I think it's a pointless exercise asking for team players. Has anyone ever attended an interview and claimed to be hopeless at working with other people?

I remain a capable, enthusiastic, honest person in need of a job even if some of the enthusiasm has rubbed off

How much does the position pay?

I can't work weekends.

It's the only two days I get to see my daughter.

Raymond

| Delete | Reply ▾ | Forward ▾ | Spam | Move... ▾ |

Subject:	RE: Gumtree advert
Date:	Tue, 22 Aug 2006 12:30:15 +0100
From:	"JoJo at innocent" <jojo@innocentdrinks.co.uk>
To:	"raymond delauney" <raymonddelauney@yahoo.co.uk>

Hello Raymond

Thank you for your email and for your views. We always appreciate feedback.

We don't release salaries to candidates, however we can tell you that there is no specific salary for this job. We do work within a loose salary bracket but the actual salary would depend on the skills and experience you would bring to this role. In this way we keep everything nice and flexible to help find the perfect person.

It would be great if you could send your CV and covering letter as specified on the website: www.innocentdrinks.co.uk/apply – we cannot consider any applications without seeing these first.

Bye for now

Jo
people helper
innocent
3 The Goldhawk Estate
Brackenbury Road
London
W6 0BA
jojo@innocentdrinks.co.uk

----

pomegranates and raspberries is back by popular demand.
get it while you can.
www.innocentdrinks.co.uk/guest

Date:	Tue, 22 Aug 2006 15:52:32 +0100 (BST)
From:	"raymond delauney" <raymonddelauney@yahoo.co.uk>
Subject:	RE: Gumtree advert
To:	"JoJo at Innocent" <jojo@innocentdrinks.co.uk>

Jojo,

What do you mean there is 'no specific salary for this job'.

I'm not sure about the 'loose salary bracket' either.

Sounds like mumbo jumbo to me. The only things I like loose are my boxer shorts and girlfriends.

If you can just give me a little bit of a clue as to where the bracket starts and ends then I can make a swift decision as to whether it would be worth banging out a CV.

I haven't had the need for one as for the last two years I have been running a restaurant – into the ground as it turned out. I don't want to spend ages writing one to be told the money demands don't tally.

By the way, your job title – 'People Helper' – it really is quite awful.

No offence. Do you get a company car – a people carrier maybe?

Seriously, JoJo I could use a break here. If you could let me know what kind of jobs are on offer and what needs to be said to get an 'in' I'd be very grateful.

Thanks,

Raymond Delauney

| Delete | Reply ˅ | Forward ˅ | Spam | Move... ˅ |

Subject:	RE: Gumtree advert
Date:	Tue, 22 Aug 2006 16:41:24 +0100
From:	"JoJo at innocent" <jojo@innocentdrinks.co.uk>
To:	"raymond delauney" <raymonddelauney@yahoo.co.uk> CC: "Karen at innocent"

Hello Raymond

I'm sorry but I can't give you any more information on the role. All details can be found at www.innocentdrinks.co.uk/jobs.

Jo

people helper

innocent

3 The Goldhawk Estate

Brackenbury Road

London

W6 0BA

jojo@innocentdrinks.co.uk

----

pomegranates and raspberries is back by popular demand.

get it while you can.

www.innocentdrinks.co.uk/guest

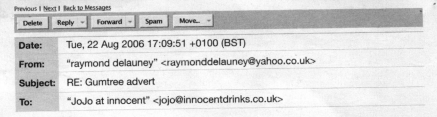

Date:	Tue, 22 Aug 2006 17:09:51 +0100 (BST)
From:	"raymond delauney" <raymonddelauney@yahoo.co.uk>
Subject:	RE: Gumtree advert
To:	"JoJo at innocent" <jojo@innocentdrinks.co.uk>

JoJo,

How can you be a 'people helper' if you don't help people?

I looked at the website and there's nothing there about what celery people are on.

All I want is a job that pays okay and this fruit juice thing sounds like it might be the one.

Are there any jobs for around £30k?

This is the minimum I can accept as I have to pay the ex-wife most of that.

Is it right to capitalise the third letter in your first name? I don't think it is.

How much does your job pay? Sounds like an easy enough number.

Have you got any influence as to who gets the jobs?

Please help.

Raymond

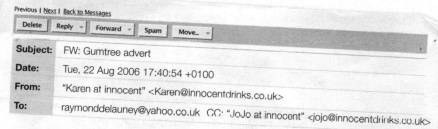

Subject:	FW: Gumtree advert
Date:	Tue, 22 Aug 2006 17:40:54 +0100
From:	"Karen at innocent" <Karen@innocentdrinks.co.uk>
To:	raymonddelauney@yahoo.co.uk CC: "JoJo at innocent" <jojo@innocentdrinks.co.uk>

Hello Raymond,

I have had a look through the email exchange between yourself and Jo, who is a member of my team, and would ask that we bring this conversation to an end. We are always delighted to hear from talented, positive people who understand our brand. I am not, however, happy with the tone or content of your mails.

Thank you

Karen

UK People Leader

Date: Thu, 24 Aug 2006 10:18:01 +0100 (BST)

From: "raymond delauney" <raymonddelauney@yahoo.co.uk>

Subject: RE: Gumtree advert

To: "Karen at innocent" <Karen@innocentdrinks.co.uk>

Hello Karen,

I have just read your rather haughty mail and I have to say I feel violated.

I applied to a 'people helper' only to be reported to a 'people leader' then effectively told I am not talented or positive. This is insulting and I fail to see how it is helping people.

I want and need a job. And I expect a level of respect, is that too much to ask?

It's not that I have difficulty in 'understanding the brand' it's just that I don't agree with some of your strategy. You have to take the rough with the smoothie, so to speak.

Do you think it's possible to work for a company and yet hold an independent, dissenting voice or do you simply want a bunch of 'Yes' men who toe the company line? It seems the answer is yes.

I am not afraid to speak my mind. When I worked for Express Dairies I told the chairman to his face that I disapproved of the working conditions I, and everyone else, was forced to endure.

I further pointed out exactly the reasons why. All my colleagues moaned behind his back – and that's all they did. The chairman said to my face that I had 'the balls to stand up for myself' – and he told me that he respected that.

Changes were made as a result of me voicing my opinions and even though, once my month trial period ended, I was not offered a full time contract at least I felt I made a difference for others.

I have a good background in marketing, successfully advertising my own (restaurant) business before events conspired against me and forced it to close due to lack of trade.

I honestly think I could be of use to your company in this area. My chief skill would be marketing. I'm good at spotting glaring mistakes. For example, I notice JoJo signs off her mails with the words *'pomegranates and raspberries is back by popular demand. Get it while you can'*.

Do you seriously think on reading this I or anyone else will drop everything, dash to the nearest shop, hurriedly hand over a couple of quid and swill down the contents of a pomegranate drink? I don't think so – not even if the statement is highlighted in red.

My **strategy** would be less obvious and more effective. The health angle is the obvious route to navigate to my mind, perhaps with the whiff of a suggestion that guzzling said juice will prevent and, in some instances, eradicate serious ailments.

How about – **'Pomegranates and raspberries eases the pain of piles'**

I don't see how I could have upset your colleague by enquiring how much the job pays.

What's the big secret? People work for money and they need to know how much is up for grabs before they sit down for an interview. I'm not getting my suit dry cleaned and travelling half way across London only to be told the job is £12,000 a year and my boss is a 19-year-old kid wearing a name badge declaring himself 'Raymond's Superior'

I would like to know what marketing jobs are on offer in your company and the exact amount they pay. Could you also send holiday entitlement and a full list of perks. Is this an outrageous demand?

Regards,

Raymond

Delete | Reply | Forward | Spam | Move

Subject:	Out of Office AutoReply: Gumtree advert
Date:	Thu, 24 Aug 2006 10:18:30 +0100
From:	"Karen at innocent" <Karen@innocentdrinks.co.uk>
To:	"raymond delauney" <raymonddelauney@yahoo.co.uk>

Thank you for your email. I am out of the office today back in tomorrow. I will get back to you as soon as possible.

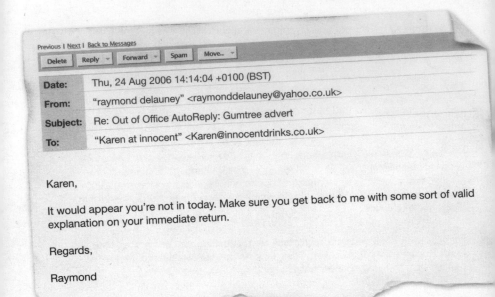

Delete | Reply ▾ | Forward ▾ | Spam | Move... ▾

Date:	Thu, 24 Aug 2006 14:14:04 +0100 (BST)
From:	"raymond delauney" <raymonddelauney@yahoo.co.uk>
Subject:	Re: Out of Office AutoReply: Gumtree advert
To:	"Karen at innocent" <Karen@innocentdrinks.co.uk>

Karen,

It would appear you're not in today. Make sure you get back to me with some sort of valid explanation on your immediate return.

Regards,

Raymond

NO REPLY

THE LUNCHBOX

Young award-winning company is looking for key member of the team to lead our kitchen brigade. You must have a passion, energy and belief that healthy ethical food can taste good, as this is what our company is all about.

You must be comfortable in the kitchen but most importantly willing to lead a team and organise a department. Formal training a bonus but not necessary.

A fantastic opportunity to work in The Big Lunchbox at its new location.

For more information about our company please look to our website www.biglunchbox.co.uk. If you are interested please email me anita@biglunchbox.co.uk

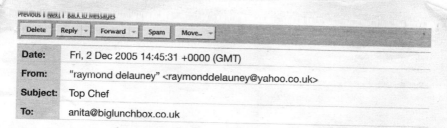

Delete   Reply ▾   Forward ▾   Spam   Move... ▾

Date:	Fri, 2 Dec 2005 14:45:31 +0000 (GMT)
From:	"raymond delauney" <raymonddelauney@yahoo.co.uk>
Subject:	Top Chef
To:	anita@biglunchbox.co.uk

Hi,

One of my people saw the ad.

Why don't you blasted people put down the salary when you advertise for applicants?

Do you require someone who can flip burgers or a master chef at the top of his trade?

Someone who is capable of whipping up a feast with a pair of eggs, a sprig of parsley, red onion, a slither of mozzarella, olive oil and some fennel seed.

I might be interested – if the price is right.

The question is do you have enough money to secure my services?

I can make food look good, taste wonderful and smell enticing. Mostly by using eggs.

Get back down to me with a figure pertaining to your budget and I'll decide if I wish to further pursue my application.

I'm told my Rondelle of Salmon in juniper berry sauce more than compensates for my brusque manner.

I'd be more than willing to prepare the above meal (my signature dish) for you as a trial. If you are good looking we could do this at my place. I am newly divorced.

Raymond

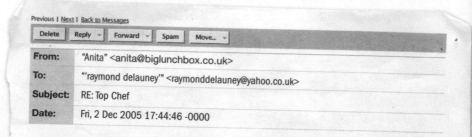

| Delete | Reply ▼ | Forward ▼ | Spam | Move... ▼ |

From:	"Anita" <anita@biglunchbox.co.uk>
To:	"'raymond delauney'" <raymonddelauney@yahoo.co.uk>
Subject:	RE: Top Chef
Date:	Fri, 2 Dec 2005 17:44:46 -0000

What are your salary expectations?

| Delete | Reply ▼ | Forward ▼ | Spam | Move... ▼ |

Date:	Fri, 2 Dec 2005 18:01:07 +0000 (GMT)
From:	"raymond delauney" <raymonddelauney@yahoo.co.uk>
Subject:	RE: Top Chef
To:	"Anita" <anita@biglunchbox.co.uk>

Hey,

We could start the mail like this:

How are you Raymond?

Thanks for showing an interest in the job on offer.

Never mind the niceties, I'm often told my manner is to the point – when you are a chef you have no time to waste. So I'll forgive you your insolence.

Here's an idea:

When you post up an advert you might consider posting the actual salary on offer. That way we can avoid this wasteful ping ponging of mails.

I'm slap bang in the middle of preparing a thinly sliced Norcia ham with fresh black figs in a herb salad.

Just tell me how much you can afford. Surely that can't be too difficult, honey glaze.

I've a feeling I might be way off your radar when it comes to how much you can afford.

It all depends on what you want – a busy restaurant with good food or a burger spinner – if you want the best, and I am that person – It costs.

That deal is still on for a free dinner depending on your weight/height ratio.

The ex wife was a bit of a porker and I'm downsizing.

Best regards,

Raymond Delauney

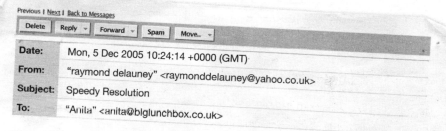

| Delete | Reply ▾ | Forward ▾ | Spam | Move... ▾ |

Date:	Mon, 5 Dec 2005 10:24:14 +0000 (GMT)
From:	"raymond delauney" <raymonddelauney@yahoo.co.uk>
Subject:	Speedy Resolution
To:	"Anita" <anita@biglunchbox.co.uk>

Anita,

I've put a couple of offers on the back gas ring whilst I wait for you to unveil your package proposal.

Do you guys offfer BUPA? I'd be loath to relinquish that perk.

I assembled a chocolate Ganache Meringue to die for yesterday.

Raymond

Delete | Reply ▾ | Forward ▾ | Spam | Move... ▾

Date:	Wed, 7 Dec 2005 10:11:49 +0000 (GMT)
From:	"raymond delauney" <raymonddelauney@yahoo.co.uk>
Subject:	RE: Top Chef
To:	"Anita" <anita@biglunchbox.co.uk>

Anita,

Are you offering me the job or what?

Get back to me today with some sort of proposal or else I'm withdrawing my interest.

Raymond Delauney

Delete | Reply ▾ | Forward ▾ | Spam | Move... ▾

Date:	Thu, 8 Dec 2005 12:04:36 +0000 (GMT)
From:	"raymond delauney" <raymonddelauney@yahoo.co.uk>
Subject:	RE: Top Chef
To:	"Anita" <anita@biglunchbox.co.uk>

ANITA.

That's it. My patience has finally run out.

I'd love to prepare a custard pie and place it firmly in your face for wasting my time.

MESSER.

END OF CORRESPONDENCE

RUGBY INVENTION

Delete | Reply ⌄ | Forward ⌄ | Spam | Move... ⌄

Date:	Mon, 28 Nov 2005 10:21:14 +0000 (GMT)
From:	"raymond delauney" <raymonddelauney@yahoo.co.uk>
Subject:	Brilliant Idea!
To:	janet.moyes@ft-ones.com

Good Day,

Would you want to invest in this idea? It is an absolute winner!

I have a pioneering scheme so devilishly ingenious that once patented will not only earn me a considerable fortune but will also help the England rugby team retain the World Cup in 2007.

I am aware that's a big claim with the All Blacks swatting everything that obstructs their path however with a little help from me and the prudent appliance of science I believe we can overcome any tactic the southern hemisphere teams can chuck at us.

My first objective is personal affluence; I make no bones about that.

I was forced to give up playing rugby early on in my career. Not through any form of debilitating injury but simply because I found the game too brutal for my body. I only weigh 8 stone in my raincoat and have to run around in the shower to get wet. My slight frame hasn't prevented me watching from the sidelines examining skills and strategies.

For the best part of the last ten years I have been spending between 2–3 hours throwing a rugby ball in my back garden.

I have developed and advanced my technique to what it is in its present form – the finished article.

In a nutshell as I sprint with the ball in hand toward the opposition (I use cardboard cut outs in my garden) I shape to throw to my right with my entire body twisting in that direction. I have manufactured a complicated technique that makes the ball squirt out deceptively to the left. I get a consistent 15–20 yards distance through a hanging tyre. And I am a man in my early seventies.

This skill has taken years to master. I fully believe this dexterity could be taught to a professional rugby player with the aid of my DVD in a matter of some 12–14 weeks.

I have written to Jonny Wilkinson who is 'intrigued' by the idea and would like to learn more. He has already signed a Non Disclosure Agreement and I hope to begin tutoring him once he recovers from an operation on his groin.

My dream is to see Jonny unveil the technique on the biggest stage of all, in the later rounds of the World Cup, preferably edging out the All Blacks in the final!

On the back of this success I want to sell my DVD to the wider public. Jonny will have effectively marketed it for me by this time. Ideally I'd like to be filmed as the teacher however I might agree to Jonny doing it as I will undergo a hip replacement operation at some point next year.

Could you please advise me first of your reaction and how best to go about patenting this gem of an idea?

Thanks in advance,

Raymond Delauney

Previous | Next | Back to Messages

| Delete | Reply ▾ | Forward ▾ | Spam | Move... ▾ |

From:	"Ronald Webb" <webbronald@hotmail.com>
To:	raymonddelauney@yahoo.co.uk
Subject:	Rugby
Date:	Mon, 28 Nov 2005 11:48:16 +0000

Dear Sir,

I have read with interest the press release concerning new rugby ball handling techniques. Do you have any film or proof of your techniques that is available online?

Yours faithfully,

Ronald Webb

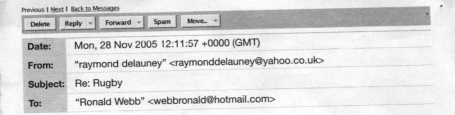

Date:	Mon, 28 Nov 2005 12:11:57 +0000 (GMT)
From:	"raymond delauney" <raymonddelauney@yahoo.co.uk>
Subject:	Re: Rugby
To:	"Ronald Webb" <webbronald@hotmail.com>

Ronald,

Thanks for getting back to me.

Your swift response would indicate both efficiency and curiosity on your part. All credit to you for possessing these two fine qualities. I sense though that you require some re-assurance as to the skills I boast of.

I can provide you this.

I've spent the best part of the last ten years camped in my cramped back garden in all weathers flinging, hurling, chucking and tossing rugby balls through a tyre hanging from an oak tree.

My 'obsessive behaviour' was even mentioned in the divorce papers served on me by my now estranged wife. So I'd like to think I haven't been wasting my time.

By employing complicated mathematical formulas (I was a maths tutor for 12 years before being forced out of the profession), and factoring in critical elements such as rotation and twist, trajectory, climatic conditions and the obvious slight displacement of surface rubber I can move a rugby ball like no other.

I can throw the oval shaped object in such a way that will not only change the game of rugby as we know it but, I believe, introduce standard and accepted strategies beyond my lifetime. Hopefully my legacy will be known as the 'Delauney Move'.

The pass requires exceptional dexterity, speed of arm, good hand/eye co-ordination and a small measure of double jointedness.

Wilko (Jonny Wilkinson) has sent me a text message saying he was 'absolutely flabbergasted' at what I can do with a ball and wants to meet me at his earliest inconvenience. He has seen video footage of my various passes.

As I understand it our meeting will take place after an operation on his groin. I don't think I have to remind you of the exceptional marketability Jonny possesses.

The way I can manipulate a rugby ball cannot be taught overnight, however with the aid of a DVD, perseverance and quite possibly a plastic arm brace (which we sell with the DVD) a similar action could be learnt within three months.

Someone of Jonny's ability should pick things up a good deal more quickly – with perhaps as little as six weeks of intensive training.

I can envisage schools across the world (particularly in New Zealand) teaching the Delauney Move to eager children willing to learn the magical secrets of my craft.

The question is Ronald, do you wish to board this historic, lavish money making journey I plan to embark on?

Please let me know if you wish to pursue this matter further.

Best regards,

Raymond Delauney

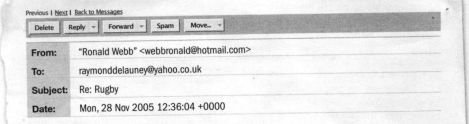

Delete	Reply ⌄	Forward ⌄	Spam	Move... ⌄

From:	"Ronald Webb" <webbronald@hotmail.com>
To:	raymonddelauney@yahoo.co.uk
Subject:	Re: Rugby
Date:	Mon, 28 Nov 2005 12:36:04 +0000

Mr Delauney,

Thank you for your equally swift reply. A man with time to spare and on his hands is indeed a precious commodity in this day and age.

My enquiries into your patented Delauney move are as much concerned with copyright infringement as they are with financial investment.

I myself hail from Australia (Lush Melbourne) where I spent the business end of my 40s working for the Australian Patents Office.

This was the 1970s – a period of frenzied creativity in the Southern Hemisphere's arts and sciences.

Of the thousands of patents that passed through my hands was an application from a Mr Jo Washora of New South Wales. He was an Aboriginal Gentleman. (Are we allowed to say Aboriginal in this fallen age, or need I step aboard the PC Bandwagon and call him Brown?) seeking to patent the 'Washora Fizzer', a technique whereby he could propel an Australian Football to the right, while feigning to throw it to the left.

The patent indeed materialised and I know that Mr Washora found some success with his technique in the Australian football league, where he was employed as a freelance coach, much like Kevin Costner's Crash Davies character in Bull Durham.

My concerns regarding your technique are twofold. One – the sport is Rugby, as opposed to AFL, but it is debatable as to whether the patent could be isolated to a separate pastime. And two – your technique flights the ball from right to left, the opposite of Mr Washora but (as I'm sure you will appreciate) unnervingly similar. You may also find that, if you tried your technique in Australia, the ball would spin in the opposite direction, much as bath water does down a plug hole. If that were to be the case, you would be in direct contravention of Australian patent law, and would face a severe fine and/or modest prison sentence.

My question must therefore be, Sir, whether you have yet entered the grim arena of international patents?

Yours,

Mr Webb

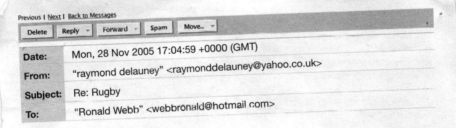

| Delete | Reply ▾ | Forward ▾ | Spam | Move.. ▾ |

Date:	Mon, 28 Nov 2005 17:04:59 +0000 (GMT)
From:	"raymond delauney" <raymonddelauney@yahoo.co.uk>
Subject:	Re: Rugby
To:	"Ronald Webb" <webbronald@hotmail.com>

Ronald,

Many thanks for explaining the state of play so comprehensively in your last mail.

I don't mind you Australians so much. A straight talking breed and there's much to be said for that.

Some of your fellow blighters might still shoulder a chip about the way our ancestors treated your forefathers and I personally find the whole Gallipoli bleating in especially rotten taste. Sending squaddies to their pointless slaughter was an accepted code of conduct during the so-called Great War. It's not as if thousands more Brits didn't suffer needless deaths themselves.

My father apparently deserted his post at the front in 1916. He was court martialled in his absence then sentenced to be shot in his absence. He told them they could shoot him in his absence!

I'm sorry but I really can't let this missive go without mentioning how brilliant it was tanning your backsides during the Ashes! I spent 18 months in the fifties trying to affect reverse swing with the new ball through the use of glycerine – but don't get me started on that.

Let's get down to brass tacks:

There can't be too many people in the patent business who've heard of the Washora Fizzer. I must admit to being put out by the arrival of this distressing revelation.

Not simply because someone beat me to the draw, not just because it now appears I might have wasted the last 10 years of my life mucking about in the back garden whilst my marriage disintegrated. No, I'm more narked that this Aborigine has conjured up a snazzier name in the 'Washora Fizzer' than my blandly titled 'Delauney Move'.

The only patent I know anything about is the bet of the same name – one treble, three singles and three doubles. After years of backing a variety of four legged creatures via this method it is patently obvious to me that this is a bloody bad bet.

Is this Washora fellow still alive? If he were dead would it benefit me? I'm not suggesting foul play here, just trying to establish and re-evaluate my position.

I've only one other project on the backburner. I'm in the process of developing a new form of snooker chalk that doesn't make the cue ball 'kick' when struck. I'm not sure if there is a big enough market for this or whether it even reduces the kick at all. Tests have proven erratic so far as I've only been on the case for 6 months.

Do you know if anything like this is on the market?

Best regards,

Raymond Delauney

NO REPLY

ASS-EASE

Delete | Reply ▾ | Forward ▾ | Spam | Move... ▾

Date:	Thu, 8 Dec 2005 15:47:45 +0000 (GMT)
From:	"raymond delauney" <raymonddelauney@yahoo.co.uk>
Subject:	Congratulations!
To:	annie.james@the-tabloid.co.uk.

Annie,

Congratulations on being made Editor of Health features in The Tabloid newspaper. Way to go!

Here's your first scoop.

I have something here that may be of extreme interest to you and your new colleagues. Indeed it may possibly gain you an early pay rise!

I'm essentially a doctor out of Tucson, Arizona who has invented a revolutionary new health product that is currently taking the States by storm. I'm here in Britain to publicise the product and catch a bit of the culture you cockney guys have to offer!

My Product is called Ass-Ease in the States and will shortly be marketed here but under a different name. **"My ambition is to make the fat ass a thing of the past".**

Every slimming survey undertaken tells us the same thing – that the part of the body a woman is most dissatisfied with is her ass (or 'arse' as you English guys call it).

Obesity has reached epidemic proportions back home. Sure, being fat is caused primarily by what you eat and how often you exercise, however the single most important factor on what size jeans you wear concerns the genes you were born with.

Simply put some people gain weight easily and some don't.

During the past 20 years I have studied the people of Newfoundland, Canada. Geographically isolated from the rest of Canada, Newfoundland has seen limited migration. Most of the island's 500,000 settlers can trace their ancestry to the original 20,000 settlers.

The body fat percentage in Newfoundland is remarkably low with the average ass there being skinnier than, say, an ass in Florida.

I have spent the best part of my life researching the 'skinny gene' and used my findings to produce my own unique product. Results in the US have been phenomenal. Below are some authentic letters I have received.

"Hi Professor Delauney, thanks to your awesome product my wife's ass is back to the size it was when I married it!"

Doyle Hanson, Mississippi

"At first I wasn't sure to believe if ASS-EASE actually worked but I've lost a good 8 pounds on my fanny. Do you have any other products for arm fat?"

Shana Roberts, California

"ASS-EASE is the perfect gift for the person who wants to slip inside that pair of jeans they can't get into anymore."

Phil Robertie, New Jersey

Annie, I would be more than willing to let you have a free sample of my kit for review.

I don't know the dimensions of your butt but I bet it could do with some trimming! No offence.

I would offer you **ASS-EASE** for as long as you wanted or needed it (not long after the first course of treatments).

Please could you get back to me Annie with some sort of decision either way? I am eager to push on with the marketing of my product

No BIG Butts – mail me!

Please let me know your immediate reaction before I approach any other publicists. I'm keen to give you first scoop!

Best regards,

Doctor Raymond Delauney M.D., Ph.D

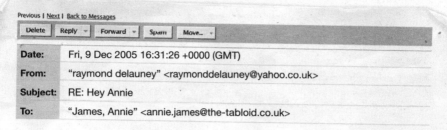

Date:	Fri, 9 Dec 2005 16:31:26 +0000 (GMT)
From:	"raymond delauney" <raymonddelauney@yahoo.co.uk>
Subject:	RE: Hey Annie
To:	"James, Annie" <annie.james@the-tabloid.co.uk>

Annie,

What is your initial reaction?

No need for sugar coating.

Do you not think this is what the 21st century woman finally wants?

This is HUGE and I want you to be part of it.

Raymond

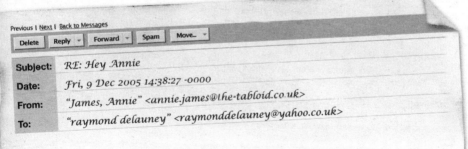

Subject:	RE: Hey Annie
Date:	Fri, 9 Dec 2005 14:38:27 -0000
From:	"James, Annie" <annie.james@the-tabloid.co.uk>
To:	"raymond delauney" <raymonddelauney@yahoo.co.uk>

Hi,

What product – sorry if you have already emailed about this, but it's been a busy week!

Thanks,

Annie

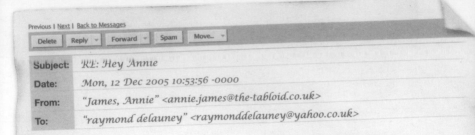

Delete | Reply ▾ | Forward ▾ | Spam | Move... ▾

Subject:	RE: Hey Annie
Date:	Mon, 12 Dec 2005 10:53:56 -0000
From:	"James, Annie" <annie.james@the-tabloid.co.uk>
To:	"raymond delauney" <raymonddelauney@yahoo.co.uk>

Not sure we're going to run with this on this occasion. Good luck with it though.

Many thanks

Annie

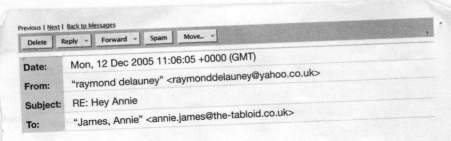

Delete | Reply ▾ | Forward ▾ | Spam | Move... ▾

Date:	Mon, 12 Dec 2005 11:06:05 +0000 (GMT)
From:	"raymond delauney" <raymonddelauney@yahoo.co.uk>
Subject:	RE: Hey Annie
To:	"James, Annie" <annie.james@the-tabloid.co.uk>

Annie,

I appreciate your reply on this one even though it is negative at present.

So many people lack common courtesy these days, even you Brits, which has surprised me a little.

My wife has lost 4 pounds on her ass since I administered the treatment. Basically, I got the ass back I married.

Listen, I don't know how big your ass is or even if it's overweight. Hopefully not but bear in mind an oversized butt is the most disliked part of a woman's body and the area of the body a man most admires (including gay men).

If you're carrying some surplus butt flesh then I'd love to work on it for you personally, absolutely free of charge.

If you are okay ass wise then I could conduct the experiment on some of the other girls in the office. We could photograph the asses before and after.

I'm in my office all morning, afternoon I'm injecting solid (asses lined up from here to Big Ben) so please have a think and please, please mail me back as soon as you can.

Thanks,

Doctor Raymond Delauney

'My ambition is to make a fat ass the thing of the past.'

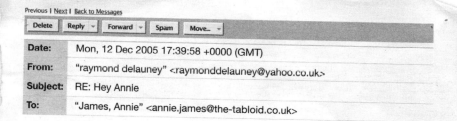

Previous I Next I Back to Messages

| Delete | Reply ⌄ | Forward ⌄ | Spam | Move... ⌄ |

Date:	Mon, 12 Dec 2005 17:39:58 +0000 (GMT)
From:	"raymond delauney" <raymonddelauney@yahoo.co.uk>
Subject:	RE: Hey Annie
To:	"James, Annie" <annie.james@the-tabloid.co.uk>

Hey Annie,

Just done injecting 35 butts this afternoon.

I'm getting though more asses than Elton John!

Sorry to hassle you but disappointed to see no response.

How about the before and after idea – we could put your ass on the line for authenticity or if it's not big we could use one of your underlings' bots.

How about it?

I could chuck a few dollars into the pot to facilitate the red tape procedure.

Doctor Raymond Delauney

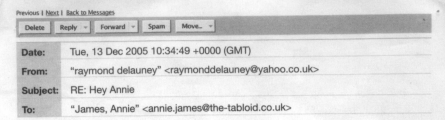

Hi Annie,

Hope you are good.

Got another production line of asses to see to all day again so grabbing five to buzz you on an update.

I sensed you weren't too keen on an **ASS-Ease** product review so how about a competition?

We could run **'Win a Slim Ass this ChristmASS' competition.**

I'll give away a free course of treatments to the Sun winner.

Would be a cool prize and maybe elevate you up the company ladder.

What do you think.

Please, please get back to me.

Your friend,

Raymond

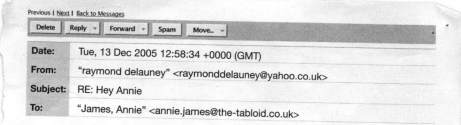

Delete	Reply ▾	Forward ▾	Spam	Move... ▾

Date:	Tue, 13 Dec 2005 12:58:34 +0000 (GMT)
From:	"raymond delauney" <raymonddelauney@yahoo.co.uk>
Subject:	RE: Hey Annie
To:	"James, Annie" <annie.james@the-tabloid.co.uk>

Hey Annie,

Just thought I'd hand you a visit to the last chance saloon.

I got a group of people called the 3 AM girls very keen to run a story – me to offer Jennifer Lopez the ASS-Ease treatment.

Buck Hudson, who runs the PR company I use, is personal friends with her, and if we can agree a fee she is prepared to endorse the product.

I think that once the British public see that J-Lo is willing to do something about her butt size then they will all want to take some positive action. We are also in talks with Beyonce – I don't think the public realise how big her butt is as it is air brushed an awful lot. Believe me when I say it is the size of Brooklyn!

I'm also issuing a challenge that if Ass-Ease is unsuccessful on any journalist I try it on I will donate $100,000 to President Blair.

I would prefer to use your paper as I'm told it is bigger and better than the XXXXXX.

Please stop ignoring me!

C'mon Annie!

Raymond

171

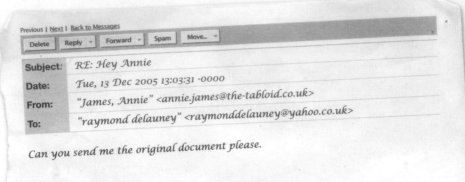

Delete | Reply ▾ | Forward ▾ | Spam | Move... ▾

Subject:	RE: Hey Annie
Date:	Tue, 13 Dec 2005 13:03:31 -0000
From:	"James, Annie" <annie.james@the-tabloid.co.uk>
To:	"raymond delauney" <raymonddelauney@yahoo.co.uk>

Can you send me the original document please.

Thanks

Annie

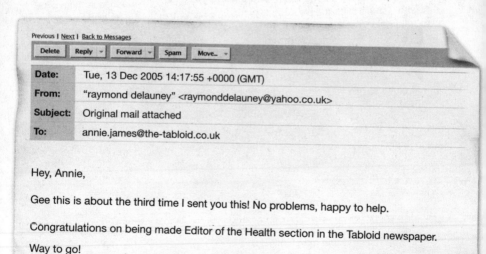

Delete | Reply ▾ | Forward ▾ | Spam | Move... ▾

Date:	Tue, 13 Dec 2005 14:17:55 +0000 (GMT)
From:	"raymond delauney" <raymonddelauney@yahoo.co.uk>
Subject:	Original mail attached
To:	annie.james@the-tabloid.co.uk

Hey, Annie,

Gee this is about the third time I sent you this! No problems, happy to help.

Congratulations on being made Editor of the Health section in the Tabloid newspaper.
Way to go!

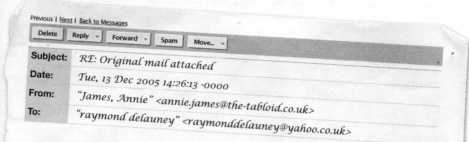

| Delete | Reply ▾ | Forward ▾ | Spam | Move... ▾ |

Subject:	RE: Original mail attached
Date:	Tue, 13 Dec 2005 14:26:13 -0000
From:	"James, Annie" <annie.james@the-tabloid.co.uk>
To:	"raymond delauney" <raymonddelauney@yahoo.co.uk>

What does it contain?

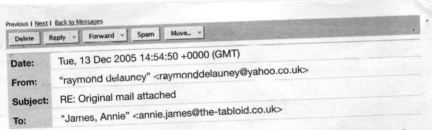

| Delete | Reply ▾ | Forward ▾ | Spam | Move... ▾ |

Date:	Tue, 13 Dec 2005 14:54:50 +0000 (GMT)
From:	"raymond delauncy" <raymonddelauney@yahoo.co.uk>
Subject:	RE: Original mail attached
To:	"James, Annie" <annie.james@the-tabloid.co.uk>

Gee, Annie has anyone ever mentioned you are pretty damn direct when it comes to conversations?

Mind you some guys like tough talking in a woman. I prefer a tidy butt and so does practically every red blooded man in the universe (minus the chubby chasers!)

A deal with J-Lo is on the table. She wants 40% of the business – greedy girl! I'll act outraged and trim that down but with her name I think that is an absolute bargain.

Okay, speed lesson in the treatment of obesity.

Drugs to treat obesity can be divided into three groups: those which reduce food intake, those which alter metabolism and those which increase thermogenesis. Monoamines acting on noradrenergic receptors, serotonin receptors, dopamine receptors and histamine receptors can reduce food intake. A number of peptides also affect food intake.

The noradrenergic drugs phentermine, diethylpropion, mazindol benzphetamine and phendimetrazine are approved only for short-term use. Sibutramine, a norepinephrine-serotonin re-uptake inhibitor, is approved for long-term use. Orlistat inhibits pancreatic lipase and can block 30% of triglyceride hydrolysis in subjects eating a 30% fat diet.

The only thermogenic drug combination that has been tested is ephedrine and caffeine, but this treatment has not been approved by regulating agencies. Leptin is currently in clinical trials and other drugs that may modulate peptide-feeding systems are being developed.

We use noradrenergic drugs in varying safe, tried and tested combinations.

Are you eager to have your ass trimmed on a trial basis?

Do you want to run a feature on us?

Will your next reply be more than one line?

Raymond

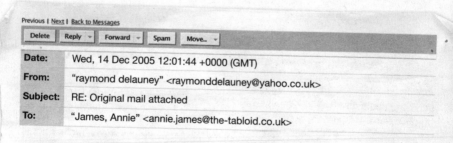

Delete   Reply ▾   Forward ▾   Spam   Move... ▾

Date:	Wed, 14 Dec 2005 12:01:44 +0000 (GMT)
From:	"raymond delauney" <raymonddelauney@yahoo.co.uk>
Subject:	RE: Original mail attached
To:	"James, Annie" <annie.james@the-tabloid.co.uk>

Hey Annie,

Anything happening your end?

As regards rear ends?

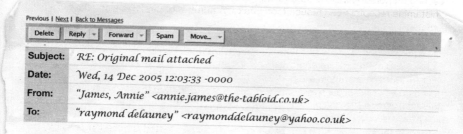

| Delete | Reply ▾ | Forward ▾ | Spam | Move... ▾ |

Subject:	RE: Original mail attached
Date:	Wed, 14 Dec 2005 12:03:33 -0000
From:	"James, Annie" <annie.james@the-tabloid.co.uk>
To:	"raymond delauney" <raymonddelauney@yahoo.co.uk>

Sorry, it's a no-goer I'm afraid – just not for us at the moment.

Annie

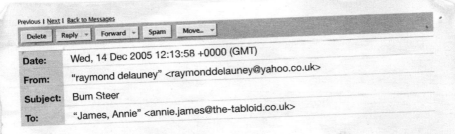

| Delete | Reply ▾ | Forward ▾ | Spam | Move... ▾ |

Date:	Wed, 14 Dec 2005 12:13:58 +0000 (GMT)
From:	"raymond delauney" <raymonddelauney@yahoo.co.uk>
Subject:	Bum Steer
To:	"James, Annie" <annie.james@the-tabloid.co.uk>

Annie,

Why the hell have you proceeded to give me the run around over the last few days?

I've told the marketing people you guys would be running a festive feature on us? This is **TOTALLY** unprofessional.

Your responses, when you can be bothered to reply, take the form of one line bursts. Frankly, it's damn rude, Annie. I thought you British guys were polite?

You wanna play hard ball with me?

Fine.

Listen, we'll just have to get down to the way things work in the US.

I'll be direct.

How much to grease your palm?

I can go up to $30,000 in juice – but **NO higher** than that, so don't squeeze me any tighter, sister.

Do not show this mail to anyone else. I ain't throwing money around like confetti. I can cc the money into any account you want within three days but I'll need some verbal assurances from you first.

I just wished that if you knew you were going to put the bite on me that you did it from day one. Now I've wasted time I haven't got. The PR department are salivating like rabid dogs.

Something longer than a one line response would be greatly appreciated.

Raymond

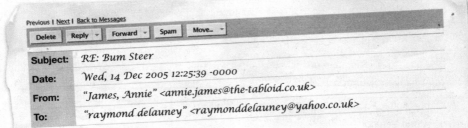

Previous I Next I Back to Messages

| Delete | Reply ▾ | Forward ▾ | Spam | Move... ▾ |

Subject:	RE: Bum Steer
Date:	Wed, 14 Dec 2005 12:25:39 -0000
From:	"James, Annie" <annie.james@the-tabloid.co.uk>
To:	"raymond delauney" <raymonddelauney@yahoo.co.uk>

Don't be ridiculous, I never said we would be running anything on this, only that I would have a look and see if it would be good for the Tabloid readership.

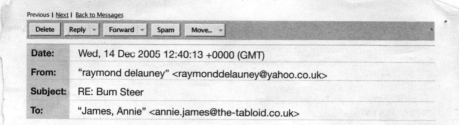

Date:	Wed, 14 Dec 2005 12:40:13 +0000 (GMT)
From:	"raymond delauney" <raymonddelauney@yahoo.co.uk>
Subject:	RE: Bum Steer
To:	"James, Annie" <annie.james@the-tabloid.co.uk>

Annie,

ARE YOU FOR REAL, SISTER?

You asked me to re-send the document NOT once but THREE times.

You then asked for more info on several occasions albeit in an astoundingly abrasive manner.

You led me up the garden path, lifted your skirt, so to speak, and then denied me what was rightfully mine.

I'm forwarding our correspondence to my legal team to see if we have enough to bind you to a contract. It might be that we have.

If I was back home in Tucson, which incidentally, is ten times better than this lousy fog infested country I'd sue your ass off never mind slim it down.

Hey, one last chance to tug at an olive branch.

$60,000 – a slim butt for you this Xmas – the one your husband married – AND 12 boxes of Cuban cigars.

C'mon Annie, I don't really want to sue your butt.

Doctor Raymond

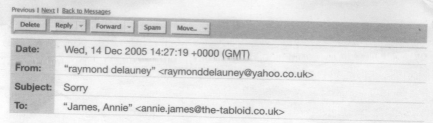

| Delete | Reply ▾ | Forward ▾ | Spam | Move... ▾ |

Date:	Wed, 14 Dec 2005 14:27:19 +0000 (GMT)
From:	"raymond delauney" <raymonddelauney@yahoo.co.uk>
Subject:	Sorry
To:	"James, Annie" <annie.james@the-tabloid.co.uk>

Annie,

Okay, maybe I got a little heated back there in my last mail.

If I did, well I apologise for that.

Listen to me Annie, and listen good.

Let's draw a line under what has already happened.

I got the PR people turning up the heat and I need to deliver now.

Just tell me how much you want. I just haven't the time to haggle any longer. If I can afford it I'll shell out. We have the funds.

Can we get anything on the front page? Not main headline of course, but maybe a pic in the corner.

I'll need to hear something back very soon or my balls will be on the block.

Happy Xmas,

Raymond

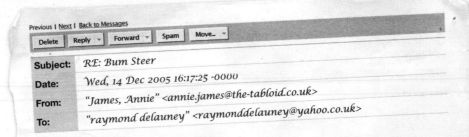

| Delete | Reply ▾ | Forward ▾ | Spam | Move... ▾ |

Subject:	RE: Bum Steer
Date:	Wed, 14 Dec 2005 16:17:25 -0000
From:	"James, Annie" <annie.james@the-tabloid.co.uk>
To:	"raymond delauney" <raymonddelauney@yahoo.co.uk>

Nothing is going on – we are not running this piece. This is the final decision.

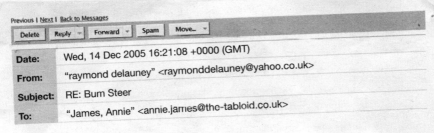

Delete | Reply | Forward | Spam | Move...

Date:	Wed, 14 Dec 2005 16:21:08 +0000 (GMT)
From:	"raymond delauney" <raymonddelauney@yahoo.co.uk>
Subject:	RE: Bum Steer
To:	"James, Annie" <annie.james@the-tabloid.co.uk>

Hamlet,

WHAT THE F....

You and your fat ass (now staying fat) have given me the runaround for long enough.

I may sue your butt off.

Tho XXXXXX are going to run with Ass-Ease anyhow.

Messer!

Raymond

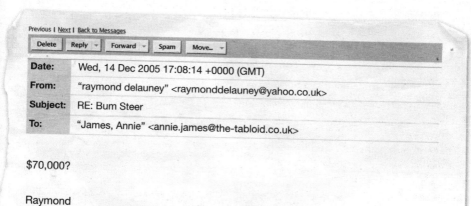

Delete | Reply | Forward | Spam | Move...

Date:	Wed, 14 Dec 2005 17:08:14 +0000 (GMT)
From:	"raymond delauney" <raymonddelauney@yahoo.co.uk>
Subject:	RE: Bum Steer
To:	"James, Annie" <annie.james@the-tabloid.co.uk>

$70,000?

Raymond

NO REPLY

CASINO

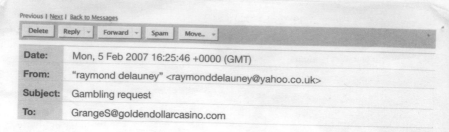

Delete | Reply ▾ | Forward ▾ | Spam | Move... ▾

Date:	Mon, 5 Feb 2007 16:25:46 +0000 (GMT)
From:	"raymond delauney" <raymonddelauney@yahoo.co.uk>
Subject:	Gambling request
To:	GrangeS@goldendollarcasino.com

Hello,

I plan to visit your casino on March 8.

I have worked six days a week for the last 9 years in a free range egg factory.

During this time I have saved £45,000 and plan to come to play in the Golden Dollar Casino and put it all on one spin of the wheel.

Would this be possible?

I would like to know if this is possible. I will not play past one spin, if I lose it's back to the egg factory and if I win I intend to move out of my mom's house and buy myself a one-bedroom flat in Margate.

Win or lose I wondered if you could comp me a three night stay in your hotel (March 8).

Best regards,

Raymond Delauney

Delete | Reply ▾ | Forward ▾ | Spam | Move... ▾

Subject:	RE: Gambling request
Date:	Fri, 9 Feb 2007 21:16:21 -0800
From:	"Grange, Sarah" <GrangeS@goldendollarcasino.com>
To:	"raymond delauney" <raymonddelauney@yahoo.co.uk>

I have forwarded this on to the folks who can answer your questions... will let you know once I hear something.

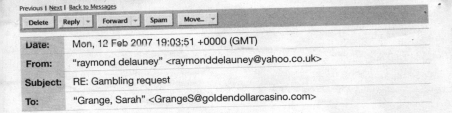

| Delete | Reply ▾ | Forward ▾ | Spam | Move... ▾ |

Date:	Mon, 12 Feb 2007 19:03:51 +0000 (GMT)
From:	"raymond delauney" <raymonddelauney@yahoo.co.uk>
Subject:	RE: Gambling request
To:	"Grange, Sarah" <GrangeS@goldendollarcasino.com>

Sarah,

Well, that was one short response.

I don't know if you read my last mail through. I stated my intention to put my
life savings – £45,000 – on one spin of the wheel. That's around 90 big ones in
American ching. What I want to know is:

a) If your joint can't handle the kind of heat I'm going to put down which casino can?
No offence, but your boys sound like a two bit outfit.

b) What is your table limit? Coins or notes?

Ideally I want one spin and out. Arrange it if you can Sarah and I'll look after you
tip wise if I win. You could even show me around town if you're under 40 and
reasonably attractive. I am single.

I think a stake of $90k is well worth three nights complimentary accommodation,
don't you?

How about this scenario? If I win I settle my own hotel bill; if I lose you comp me up?
It's basically a win/win situation for everyone – even if I do lose my life savings.

I've been dreaming about this day for the last nine years so I'm hoping for a really
good room for my stay. One that includes a kettle so that I can prepare myself a cup
of tea. I would expect the room to also have an ironing board. I will be bringing my
mother's travel iron with me. She has allowed me to borrow hers for the duration of
the holiday, as long as I promise to look after it.

If the bet comes home to roost I will be living it up, if I lose I'll still have a couple of
grand for expenses. So either way I will be able to slip you some cash for looking
after me.

Mother doesn't allow lady friends to stay over at her house so I intend to take
advantage of my stay and acquaint myself with a number of 'temporary' girlfriends.
Any discreet information facilitating this operation would be gratefully received.

Bets regards,

Raymond

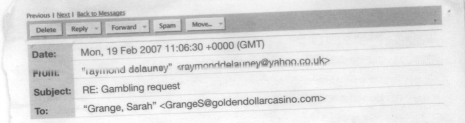

Date:	Mon, 19 Feb 2007 11:06:30 +0000 (GMT)
From:	"raymond delauney" <raymonddelauney@yahoo.co.uk>
Subject:	RE: Gambling request
To:	"Grange, Sarah" <GrangeS@goldendollarcasino.com>

Sarah,

Just to let you know unless I hear back from you today I shall book in elsewhere where my custom is appreciated. I feel I have been treated disgracefully.

I would, however, still be prepared to go out on a date during my stay.

I'll pay for the meal if you look hot.

Best regards,

Raymond Delauney

Subject:	RE: Gambling request
Date:	Tue, 20 Feb 2007 11:52:30 -0800
From:	"Grange, Sarah" <GrangeS@goldendollarcasino.com>
To:	"raymond delauney" <raymonddelauney@yahoo.co.uk>

We attempted to send you 4 emails pertaining to your request which came back undeliverable. Therefore I am having Ms. Grange forward you the basic content and in light of your last emails you should not further correspond with anyone in our organization.

We must not only respectfully decline your request to place your proposed wager at one of our hotels; we would further not encourage such reckless behavior at all.

Our table limits are not the issue. We strictly adhere to a Code of Conduct which has been developed, in part, through our long standing relationship with the National Center for Responsible Gaming. The wager you are proposing is simply not a responsible use of your assets.

Will Wharton. General Counsel.

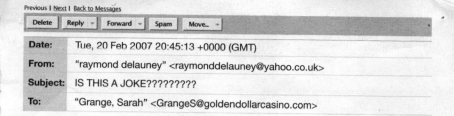

Delete | Reply ▾ | Forward ▾ | Spam | Move... ▾

Date:	Tue, 20 Feb 2007 20:45:13 +0000 (GMT)
From:	"raymond delauney" <raymonddelauney@yahoo.co.uk>
Subject:	IS THIS A JOKE?????????
To:	"Grange, Sarah" <GrangeS@goldendollarcasino.com>

Is this a joke?

I don't know what your problem is, but I bet it's hard to pronounce.

I've just got a mail from someone called Will Wharton (do what?) from Sarah Grange's mail address?

If you did attempt to send me a mail earlier (which I very much doubt) I can only suggest that any future correspondence you consider sending should first be checked to see if you have the correct spelling.

It's generally a good idea to do this before pressing the send button. You probably sent them to the .com address and not the co.uk.

When the first mail bounced back it may have provided you a vital clue you had the wrong address. Anyone with half a brain wouldn't scratch their melon and keep sending until all four messages rebounded back.

Not the village idiot in Vegas, though, just my luck to find him.

If you take your argument to its logical conclusion, and let's face it Will, I doubt you ever have, you might as well shut down your casino because your very existence costs people money. People win all the time – they just don't leave winning.

Well, I will.

You know that plan only works over the long haul. I aim to hit and run – and you don't like that. I've outsmarted you.

I'll try being nicer if you'll try being smarter.

If I want to stick my savings on one spin of the wheel how is that any different to losing it over the course of a night with smaller stakes?

Let me know your maximum table limit. You can't stop me playing. I intend to visit your casino and it is my intention to hit your Mickey Mouse establishment hard.

I'll break you and your two bob joint for some big bucks and take them back to

183

Blighty to spend.

I really can't believe this. Have you thought about renting the space in your head? It could be profitable.

If you want to go head to head with me over a game of poker instead I'll be more than willing, Will. I'm a very tasty player.

Listen, just get back to me with the facts and lose the hoity toity attitude. I'll still tip you a few bills if I feel I've been looked after during my stay.

But not before I've taken your paymaster's smash and spent it on some high-class hookers. Do you know any you could recommend?

Black and busty is my preference.

Raymond Delauney

END OF CORRESPONDENCE

JEREMY CLARKSON

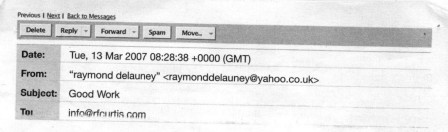

Previous | Next | Back to Messages

Delete   Reply ▾   Forward ▾   Spam   Move... ▾

Date:	Tue, 13 Mar 2007 08:28:38 +0000 (GMT)
From:	"raymond delauney" <raymonddelauney@yahoo.co.uk>
Subject:	Good Work
To:	info@rfcurtis.com

Hi,

I see you guys sell media directories that have "comprehensive, accurate and accessible media information covering national and regional press, trade and consumer publications, broadcast and freelance writers".

That's great, please send me one.

I'm just starting out in the business. Without doubt I'll do very well.

I have no money at present however I intend to remember all the people who gave me a leg up when I was at the bottom, thinking of them fondly when I make my inevitable, inexorable rise to the top.

Please send me the directory. Regard it as a VERY shrewd investment. Remember my name – Delauney – because it and I will dominate the media scene within 10 years.

That, my friend, is a promise. Failing that I desperately need the email address of Jeremy Clarkson.

Profuse gratitude in advance,

Raymond Delauney

Delete   Reply ▾   Forward ▾   Spam   Move... ▾

From:	"Roland" <roland@rfcurtis.com>
To:	"'raymonddelauney@yahoo.co.uk'" <raymonddelauney@yahoo.co.uk>
Subject:	RE: Good Work
Date:	Tue, 13 Mar 2007 10:17:58 -0000

Hi Raymond,

Thank you very much for your email.

Although I appreciate and do not doubt your future plans I am afraid that I am unable to take up your offer of investment. Please feel free to refer to our website for full details of all our products and their prices.

If you have any further queries then please don't hesitate to contact me.

Good luck.

R.

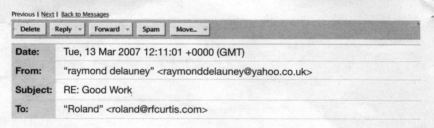

Delete   Reply ▾   Forward ▾   Spam   Move... ▾

Date:	Tue, 13 Mar 2007 12:11:01 +0000 (GMT)
From:	"raymond delauney" <raymonddelauney@yahoo.co.uk>
Subject:	RE: Good Work
To:	"Roland" <roland@rfcurtis.com>

Roland,

Thanks for your response.

You're right not to doubt my ability, determination and drive. I will make it to the top. I'll swat, swipe or schmooze my way there.

On arrival I will be well placed to remember who facilitated my journey.

Everything will be recorded in a black book.

If you scratch my back I promise to itch yours.

How about Jeremy Clarkson's email for starters and then you could possibly slip me a directory via the back door at some later date.

I could be prepared to pay a (very) reduced rate for it. Nobody will be any the wiser and I'll send for you when I'm a captain of industry.

Have a think about it.

Regards,

Raymond Delauney

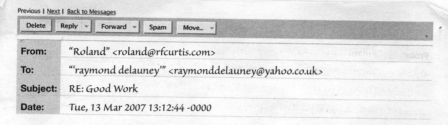

| Delete | Reply ▾ | Forward ▾ | Spam | Move... ▾ |

From:	"Roland" <roland@rfcurtis.com>
To:	"'raymond delauney'" <raymonddelauney@yahoo.co.uk>
Subject:	RE: Good Work
Date:	Tue, 13 Mar 2007 13:12:44 -0000

Hi Raymond,

Unfortunately I am unable to give out information from our products free of charge. However, I would assume that the information that you are looking for is available on the internet somewhere.

I hope this helps.

Regards,

R.

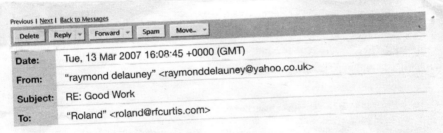

| Delete | Reply ▾ | Forward ▾ | Spam | Move... ▾ |

Date:	Tue, 13 Mar 2007 16:08:45 +0000 (GMT)
From:	"raymond delauney" <raymonddelauney@yahoo.co.uk>
Subject:	RE: Good Work
To:	"Roland" <roland@rfcurtis.com>

Roland,

Had the required info been readily available on the web as you suggest I assure you I wouldn't be hassling your good self. I have plenty of other people to hassle.

Do you want to slip me a directory in the post by 'accident'.

If this is too risky please dig out Clarkson's contact details for me – and Piers Morgan's as well. I'm arranging a charity boxing match billed as 'the Slugging Scribes – tho pen ain't as mighty as the punch'.

Should be plenty of juice in this one – and I might squeeze a little your way.

Cheers Roland

Raymond Delauney

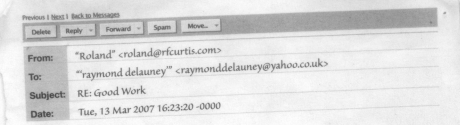

From:	"Roland" <roland@rfcurtis.com>
To:	"'raymond delauney'" <raymonddelauney@yahoo.co.uk>
Subject:	RE: Good Work
Date:	Tue, 13 Mar 2007 16:23:20 -0000

Hi Raymond,

My apologies but I really am unable to satisfy either of your requests. However, we do have a Lists Department who can create bespoke lists for you.

The minimum charge is £35 and for that you can get 20 contacts. If you would like me to get them to call you then let me know.

Regards,

R.

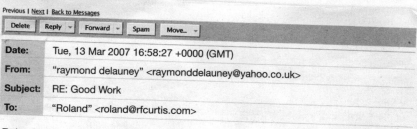

Date:	Tue, 13 Mar 2007 16:58:27 +0000 (GMT)
From:	"raymond delauney" <raymonddelauney@yahoo.co.uk>
Subject:	RE: Good Work
To:	"Roland" <roland@rfcurtis.com>

Roland,

Thanks, I'll certainly take that list of 20 as a starter. Good idea, Roland.

Can you send these to me and follow it up with an invoice. I need the address asap.

Jeremy Clarkson, Piers Morgan, Richard Branson, Roman Abramovich, Vanessa Feltz, Gary Lineker, and either woman out of Richard or Judy.

I'll have a think about the others – send these first please so I know you're not trying to pull a fast one.

Thanks,

Raymond

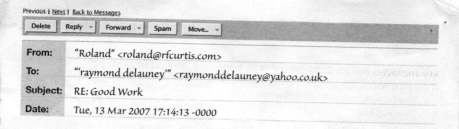

From:	"Roland" <roland@rfcurtis.com>
To:	"'raymond delauney'" <raymonddelauney@yahoo.co.uk>
Subject:	RE: Good Work
Date:	Tue, 13 Mar 2007 17:14:13 -0000

Hi Raymond,

I believe that we have our wires crossed a little here. We only list journalists and sometimes the "celebrity" journalists choose not to be listed. We don't list other "celebrities" and I think you would be hard pushed to find a company that can provide you with the contact details for the likes of Roman Abramovich.

Also on the lists side of things we work on a payment upfront basis.

One final thing, we don't pull fast ones.

Hope this helps.

Regards,

R.

189

Delete   Reply ▾   Forward ▾   Spam   Move... ▾

Date:	Tue, 13 Mar 2007 17:16:35 +0000 (GMT)
From:	"raymond delauney" <raymonddelauney@yahoo.co.uk>
Subject:	RE: Good Work
To:	"Roland" <roland@rfcurtis.com>

Roland,

The good news is I don't pull fast ones either, though I did once date a girl who ran the 400 metre hurdles for Essex Beagles. Great thighs. She left me for a javelin thrower. Ironically she was later 'chucked' by him.

I think the best way to go from here is to send over the Jez Clarkson's contact details so I know you're on the up and then I'll probably place a big order down the line.

Call it a loss leader, Roland.

You have been very pleasant to work with. I fully intend to recommend you to your superiors at some point, should you have any.

Raymond

Delete   Reply ▾   Forward ▾   Spam   Move... ▾

From:	"Roland" <roland@rfcurtis.com>
To:	"'raymond delauney'" <raymonddelauney@yahoo.co.uk>
Subject:	RE: Good Work
Date:	Tue, 13 Mar 2007 17:27:17 -0000

Hi,

I am sorry to hear about your loss. Though I still can't help I am afraid, however, I can assure you that the person's email address you are looking for is readily available on the internet and in newspapers that he writes in.

Regards,

R.

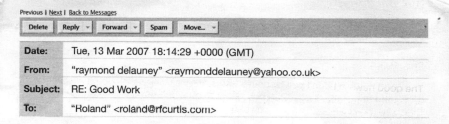

Date:	Tue, 13 Mar 2007 18:14:29 +0000 (GMT)
From:	"raymond delauney" <raymonddelauney@yahoo.co.uk>
Subject:	RE: Good Work
To:	"Roland" <roland@rfcurtis.com>

Roland,

Checked the paper but isn't in there and tried the same format as other journos but it bounced back

You are my only hope.

Would greasing your palm work out cheaper?

As mentioned I will be very rich one day. At present I'm very poor. A thousand mile journey begins with a single step. And that step is Clarko's email details.

C'mon buddy. There could be a seat on the board at stake for you here.

Remember this true story. A guy was in a jungle and he saw an elephant howling in pain. On closer inspection he noticed the creature had a thorn protruding from his hoof. He pulled it out and the elephant smiled at him and trundled off happily.

Fifteen years later the same explorer was in the same jungle and got cornered by a lion. Just as the lion was about to pounce along comes an elephant and the lion ran off.

Then the elephant crushed the explorer to death. It was a different elephant.

It's a confusing story but you catch my drift, I'm sure.

Thanks Roland, appreciate this.

Raymond

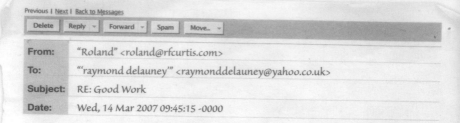

| Delete | Reply ▾ | Forward ▾ | Spam | Move... ▾ |

From:	"Roland" <roland@rfcurtis.com>
To:	"'raymond delauney'" <raymonddelauney@yahoo.co.uk>
Subject:	RE: Good Work
Date:	Wed, 14 Mar 2007 09:45:15 -0000

Morning,

Although I appreciate your generous offer of employment, I am going to have to decline I am afraid. Though if you would like to 'grease my palms' with £35 then I can get that email address over to you.

Regards,

R.

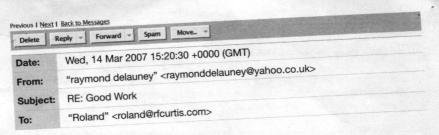

| Delete | Reply ▾ | Forward ▾ | Spam | Move... ▾ |

Date:	Wed, 14 Mar 2007 15:20:30 +0000 (GMT)
From:	"raymond delauney" <raymonddelauney@yahoo.co.uk>
Subject:	RE: Good Work
To:	"Roland" <roland@rfcurtis.com>

£35 quid for one email address?

Where's your mask?

Besides I know some of the address already. I'm sure it has a .com in it, so I should get a discount.

There's every chance Clarkson will tell me to shove it anyway so it doesn't look to be the best bit of business, even if I had that sort of money.

How about you take a peek in the directory during a tea break and then nudge it through the slips to me. I have two black books, one entitled 'Horses that owe me money' and the other named 'People I owe favours to'.

I'll stick your name in the second book.

It's a slim volume and I'm sure to look back favourably to all those encased within its binders once I'm heading up my own company.

Many thanks,

Raymond

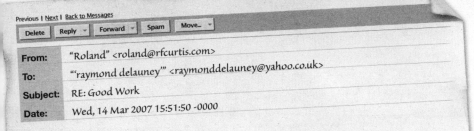

| Delete | Reply ⌄ | Forward ⌄ | Spam | Move... ⌄ |

From:	"Roland" <roland@rfcurtis.com>
To:	"'raymond delauney'" <raymonddelauney@yahoo.co.uk>
Subject:	RE: Good Work
Date:	Wed, 14 Mar 2007 15:51:50 -0000

Hi,

Apologies but I really can't do that unless you are willing to splash some cash?!?!? If not then I hope you find the information another way.

Regards,

R.

| Delete | Reply ⌄ | Forward ⌄ | Spam | Move... ⌄ |

Date:	Wed, 14 Mar 2007 16:19:31 +0000 (GMT)
From:	"Jezza Clarkson" <jezzaclarkson11@yahoo.co.uk>
Subject:	Update
To:	Roland@rfcurtis.com

Hi Jeremy Clarkson here from Top Gear,

Just back from a LandRover safari trip in Kenya. Complete waste of time, only saw four LandRovers the whole time I was there.

Just a quick note to say that all you good guys at Curtis should know this is my new email detail should anyone wish to contact me in the future.

You can have this for zero fee. In return could anyone who e-mails in asking for me today be given my old email address absolutely free of charge.

No really, I think that's fair.

Thanks,

Jeremy Clarkson

Top Gear

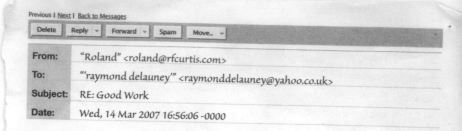

Hi Raymond,

As luck would have it Mr Clarkson has just emailed into us and said that we are allowed to pass out his details for free. He said that the old one could go out but being a professional organisation we couldn't possibly release incorrect data so therefore his new email address is jezzaclarkson11@yahoo.co.uk.

It really is extraordinary that he has emailed in at the same time as you are looking for his information. It is coincidences like this that make me see the beauty in life.

I hope this info serves you well.

Regards,

Roland

END OF CORRESPONDENCE

CAMDEN MARKET

Advertising for someone to help sell prints on a market stall in Camden.

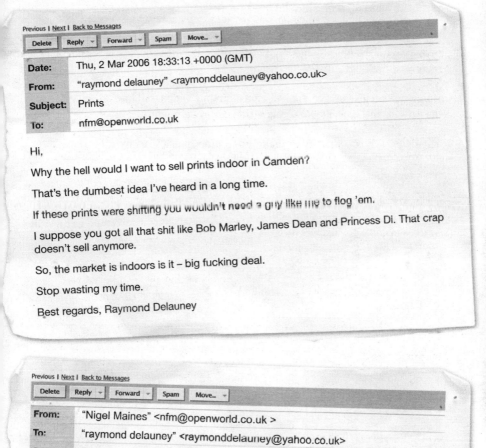

Delete Reply ▾ Forward ▾ Spam Move... ▾

Date:	Thu, 2 Mar 2006 18:33:13 +0000 (GMT)
From:	"raymond delauney" <raymonddelauney@yahoo.co.uk>
Subject:	Prints
To:	nfm@openworld.co.uk

Hi,

Why the hell would I want to sell prints indoor in Camden?

That's the dumbest idea I've heard in a long time.

If these prints were shifting you wouldn't need a guy like me to flog 'em.

I suppose you got all that shit like Bob Marley, James Dean and Princess Di. That crap doesn't sell anymore.

So, the market is indoors is it – big fucking deal.

Stop wasting my time.

Best regards, Raymond Delauney

Delete Reply ▾ Forward ▾ Spam Move... ▾

From:	"Nigel Maines" <nfm@openworld.co.uk >
To:	"raymond delauney" <raymonddelauney@yahoo.co.uk>
Subject:	Re: Prints
Date:	Thu, 2 Mar 2006 19:33:03 -0000

Is there something seriously wrong with you?

END OF CORRESPONDENCE

FOOTBALL SALES

Job description

Calling all football fans… This is an opportunity to chat about your favourite sport all day – and be paid for it!

My client is a Premiership League football club, who are looking for people to hit the phones and invite corporate/business people to some of their hospitality events.

If you have telesales experience, can maintain a high call rate, and have the proven ability to meet targets – this could be your ideal job.

This is a great opportunity to make good money in a fun environment.

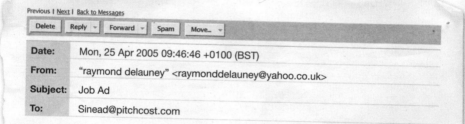

Previous | Next | Back to Messages

| Delete | Reply ▾ | Forward ▾ | Spam | Move... ▾ |

Date:	Mon, 25 Apr 2005 09:46:46 +0100 (BST)
From:	"raymond delauney" <raymonddelauney@yahoo.co.uk>
Subject:	Job Ad
To:	Sinead@pitchcost.com

Hi Sinead,

Your job ad (above) caught my eye. The one generously offering 'the opportunity to chat about your favourite sport (paragliding in my case) – *and be paid for it!*'

What an absolutely marvellous idea! To undertake a job and receive remuneration in return! This initiative might just catch on, we could call it 'work'.

I'm (safely) assuming 'chat' is a euphemism for 'sell'. Unless, of course, the position you're advertising for does actually require somebody to attend an office, phone people randomly and jaw away about the fluctuating fortunes of various football teams.

"Hi, Raymond here. You don't know me but I believe John Terry should partner Sol Campbell for England. I also believe we should play Wright-Phillips on the problematic left side. What do you think?"

"Who is this?"

Similarly, I'm presupposing you wouldn't be '*inviting*' business people to attend sporting events so much as charging them a fixed amount of money to do so. I think this is an important point of difference. Any such invitation subsequently becomes substantially less inviting after you learn you got to pay top dollar for it. Most people I know treat every pound they earn as a prisoner.

I'd like to invite you, Sinead, to the pub whereupon you can buy all my drinks. Once we'd done with the drinking I could invite you to buy me a curry. Then, to round off the night I could invite you in for coffee…

My final quibble with your advertisement involves the laughable assertion that working in a call centre and phoning up individuals who have absolutely no inclination, time or desire to 'chat' to you is – *a good way to make money in a fun environment.*

Frankly, Sinead, it isn't.

Apart from all that I think your ad is flawless.

Could you kindly send me an application form?

Relentlessly,

Raymond Delauney

Delete	Reply ▾	Forward ▾	Spam	Move.. ▾

From:	"Sinead Benson" <Sinead@pitchcost.com>
To:	"'raymond delauney'" <raymonddelauney@yahoo.co.uk>
Subject:	RE: Job Ad
Date:	Tue, 26 Apr 2005 14:06:47 +0100

Hi Raymond,

Thank you for providing me with a giggle on this very stressful day! (So much so I am only now reading yesterday's emails). Unfortunately these positions have now all been filled. But they are likely to be on the look out for more people in the coming month, so please keep an eye on our website.

Cheers,

Sinead

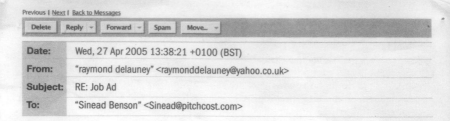

Previous | Next | Back to Messages

| Delete | Reply ▾ | Forward ▾ | Spam | Move... ▾ |

Date:	Wed, 27 Apr 2005 13:38:21 +0100 (BST)
From:	"raymond delauney" <raymonddelauney@yahoo.co.uk>
Subject:	RE: Job Ad
To:	"Sinead Benson" <Sinead@pitchcost.com>

Sinead,

I was ever so slightly saddened to hear that you endured a stressful day at work yesterday. Stress and work go hand in hand like marriage and divorce or haemorrhoids and pile cream. I consider myself fortunate that I have never suffered from stress though I have been told on more than one occasion that I am a carrier.

Perhaps you should consider resigning your current occupation and take up the position where you can chat about football all day – you get paid for it!

I just thought I'd drop you a line to notify you that it is no longer my intention to pursue this particular line of career opportunity.

I shall be marrying into money fairly shortly, hopefully later this summer. I intend to bide my time and juggle my finances until the wedding ceremony. The mere thought of work has always made me feel faintly nauseous. Ever since I've been old enough to work – I haven't.

Encouragingly, to date there has been no mention of signing a pre-nuptial agreement even though her venture capitalist father detests me with the same intensity I abhor sprouts. He suspects I am courting his daughter solely to gain access to her (his) money, which, of course, I am.

It's fair to say my fiancée is no oil painting (Edvard Munch's Scream aside) but on her debit side she has an accommodating personality, a forgiving nature and an ample bosom. She also has a two bedroomed house in Plumstead with no mortgage!

Inexorably,

Raymond Delauney

END OF CORRESPONDENCE

DPP INVENTION

| Delete | Reply ▾ | Forward ▾ | Spam | Move... ▾ |

Date:	Thu, 8 Mar 2007 15:10:45 +0000 (GMT)
From:	"raymond delauney" <raymonddelauney@yahoo.co.uk>
Subject:	Great idea for Venture Cube
To:	AlexJ@venturecube.com

Hi Alex,

I understand you guys are venture capitalists – I got something that is going to be BIG and I want you in on the ground floor with me.

My name is Raymond Delauney and I have dedicated the last four years of my life developing an extremely sophisticated piece of computer software.

After months of meticulous study, experimentation and a fair bit of tinkering I believe I now have perfected my product, which I'm calling **The DPP – Delauney Punctuation Program.**

Once my easily downloadable software is installed on your computer it automatically detects and inserts, apostrophe's, commas, full stops, exclamation marks – and anything else that it deems appropriate. It also automatically capitalises or de-capitalises any word that the user should so indicate – throughout the entire copy. The DPP is 50 times more effective and reliable than the Microsoft spell checker and works across 70 languages.

The DPP will effectively do away with the role of the sub – it's that good it can be sold to newspapers and book publishers. I would like to be known as the man who made the sub redundant. I was given my cards from the chief sub at the Mirror four years ago. Revenge is a dish best eaten, as the old saying goes.

The DPP is also programmed to recognise and downgrade 1,894 offensive swear words ranging from the lightly offensive 'berk' to the most disgusting – c**t (cunt).

It can delete the swearing completely or downgrade it – for example 'fuck' will become 'freak'.

Further, the DPP email siphon will detect and destroy mails with trigger words such as viagra, penis (when coupled with the world 'enlarge', 'enhance' and 21 variants of this word.

I can see the DPP being sold to every computer user across the land as an indispensable piece of software. If a vulture capitalist comes in with me now I will get them a great return on their money.

I have just completed eliminating all the minor technical glitches that occur when you take on a project of this size.

You interested in making some money with me?

Raymond Delauney

Previous | Next | Back to Messages

| Delete | Reply ▾ | Forward ▾ | Spam | Move.. ▾ |

Date:	Mon, 12 Mar 2007 10:57:05 +0000 (GMT)
From:	"Alex Jarvis" <AlexJ@venturecube.com>
Subject:	Re: Great Idea for Venture Cube
To:	raymonddelauney@yahoo.co.uk

Raymond,

Thanks, but this is not something we would like to pursue at this time.

Alex

P.S. It made me chuckle, but with a business like this, when you say: "it automatically detects and inserts, apostrophe's, commas..." you probably don't want the erroneous insertion of an apostrophe and a comma right there in that section of text! =)

Date:	Fri, 16 Mar 2007 12:26:54 +0000 (GMT)
From:	raymonddelauney@yahoo.co.uk
Subject:	Re: Great idea for Venture Cube
To:	"Alex Jarvis" <AlexJ@venturecube.com>

**** Auto Delete OFF ****

Alex,

I can't tell you how mad I am with my chief technician. The fuckwit (**CURSE VIOLATION: SUGGESTED ALTERNATIVE: 'FREAKWIT'**) assured me on more than one occasion that the tool had been fixed. So I mail out an entire list of vulture capitalists advertising the multifarious merits of the DPP and the dumb prick (**curse violation: suggested alternative: 'dumb idiot'**) drops a gigantic spanner in the works.

When I discovered what happened I punched the wall so hard I ended up with a battered, bloody (**CURSE VIOLATION: SUGGESTED ALTERNATIVE: 'DAMN'**) fist and a bruised ego.

I pour blood, sweat and tears into this project. Not to mention selling my holiday home in Bournemouth and the no good wanker (**CURSE VIOLATION: SUGGESTED ALTERNATIVE: 'BERK'**) screws up my entire operation by not double checking the sales pitch.

Listen, Alex, how about I take a major review of the price?

The market potential here is enormous – everyone who has a computer.

After a little bit of fine-tuning I assure you this baby will make the competition look shit (**CURSE VIOLATION: SUGGESTED ALTERNATIVE: 'FAECES'**) rate in comparison. They'll be plenty of gravy to go round.

Please have a think on this and get back to me with your immediate thought patterns.

Best regards,

Raymond Delauney

| Delete | Reply ▾ | Forward ▾ | Spam | Move... ▾ |

Date:	Mon, 19 Mar 2007 12:20:31 +0000 (GMT)
From:	"raymond delauney" <raymonddelauney@yahoo.co.uk>
Subject:	Re: Great idea for DFJ (CATCH UP)
To:	"Alex Jarvis" <AlexJ@venturecube.com>

**** Auto Delete OFF ****

Alex,

I sensed you were extremely interested in a possible investment in the DPP but only if I could iron out the odd glitches.

Those glitches have now been completely eradicated.

How would you fancy owning 50% of this soon-to-be massive company?

I'd like to talk numbers with you, big ones, I'll cut you a very generous deal, make no mistake.

The US market is something I'd like to slice up with you.

I'm holding off some big Japanese investment so get back to me pronto, please. I'll continue to hold off all investors until I hear from you.

Raymond

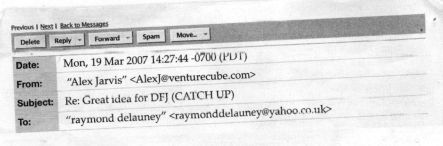

Date:	Mon, 19 Mar 2007 14:27:44 -0700 (PDT)
From:	"Alex Jarvis" <AlexJ@venturecube.com>
Subject:	Re: Great idea for DFJ (CATCH UP)
To:	"raymond delauney" <raymonddelauney@yahoo.co.uk>

**** Auto Delete ON ****

No thanks, but good luck in building the business.

END OF CORRESPONDENCE

FILMMAKER

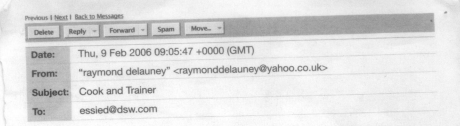

| Delete | Reply ▾ | Forward ▾ | Spam | Move... ▾ |

Date:	Thu, 9 Feb 2006 09:05:47 +0000 (GMT)
From:	"raymond delauney" <raymonddelauney@yahoo.co.uk>
Subject:	Cook and Trainer
To:	essied@dsw.com

Hi,

I saw your advertisement offering live-in cooking and training services.

Presumably you are targeting unfit, unhealthy, rich people.

I am a director of low budget movies. Occasionally I dip into working on small screen productions.

I have just finished starring in and directing a short film namely, 'I arrest you in the **Name of Delauney**', in which I break the law a staggering 100 times during the course of a thirty-day one-man crime spree.

Don't get alarmed, most of my transgressions involve breaking minor outdated statutes, however my one-man crime bender escalates throughout the course of the film, culminating in my arrest for assaulting a WPC. Other felonies include urinating in a public place, shoplifting a brown velvet suit from Moss Bros, duping an old age pensioner by pretending to fix her roof and indecently exposing myself in Harrods.

I appear before Stratford Magistrates Court for the assault on March 4th and have asked for the 99 other crimes to be taken into consideration. My solicitor advises a possible detention at Her Majesty's pleasure. This would be regrettable but make for a terrific ending for the film.

Fingers crossed, the film should premiere at the **Short Film Palme D'Or** (Cannes film festival) later this year.

You might be wondering what all this has to with you?

I wouldn't blame you for thinking that, I really wouldn't.

Hold your horses.

I have Raif Thornley-Jenkins' ear at Channel 4, he's a bigwig-commissioning editor. Raif still has a large allocation of his budget to spend on the reality show genre and has asked me for ideas.

Here's a suggestion: You could cook, clean and train me as my live-in personal trainer, whilst being followed about by a film crew. Your remit would be to get me fit. Just think about the free publicity you'd get and how it would impact on your career. Take that peculiar looking nanny on Channel 4 for an example of a career taking off.

I don't think it is inconceivable that you may get your own fitness video deal once we've canned it. I would not charge you rent during your stay and you'd have the guest bedroom. I wouldn't be able to pay you but I would chip in towards the food I consume.

We could stage part of the film, to show us rowing with each other, perhaps I cheat on my diet by sneaking downstairs in the middle of the night to eat some doughnuts in my pyjamas. What the doughnuts were doing in my pyjamas I don't know!

You follow me down the stairs and freak out whilst I scoff the doughnuts down as fast as possible before you snatch them off me. This is just a suggestion. The show will need passion, conflict and drama if it is to work. It won't succeed with just the fitness angle. That's been done before. We need more... sustenance.

Also, I expect you will probably be fit and good-looking given the nature of your job. A side theme of the film will be how I am coping with my divorce (second one). Maybe I could hit on you – this would look good for the cameras. I'm pretty fat, practically an alcoholic and take all the recreational drugs I can get my hands on, so you'd be repulsed by me – but professionally you'd still want to complete the task of getting me fit. You would have a nightly diary cam where you could break down with the stress of it all and confide to the camera how my pot belly and bad breath repulse you. Maybe we could film you putting a padlock on your bedroom door or something.

Anyway, we're storyboarding ideas at the moment so if you have any please don't hesitate to let me know. Also let me know your initial reaction and if it's the sort of thing you might be interested in.

Best regards,

Raymond Delauney

Delete   Reply ⌄   Forward ⌄   Spam   Move... ⌄

From:	"Essie Donovan" <essied@dsw.com>
To:	raymonddelauney@yahoo.co.uk
Subject:	RE: Cook and Trainer
Date:	Thu, 09 Feb 2006 09:26:11 -0800

Hello Raymond,

As tempting as it sounds I think I will decline.

I'm a little strange, I like to get paid for work I do. Call me crazy...

Sorry and good luck!

Essie D

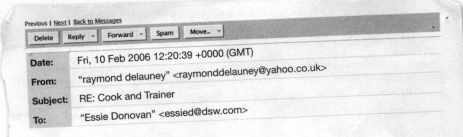

Delete   Reply ⌄   Forward ⌄   Spam   Move... ⌄

Date:	Fri, 10 Feb 2006 12:20:39 +0000 (GMT)
From:	"raymond delauney" <raymonddelauney@yahoo.co.uk>
Subject:	RE: Cook and Trainer
To:	"Essie Donovan" <essied@dsw.com>

Essie,

Are you nuts?

I just read out your mail response to my production team and all of them except the Sound Man (Curly) laughed out loud.

I'm offering you the chance to become a star and you want me to pay you big bucks on top? That's like Chantelle trying to negotiate a bumper pay deal to be stuck in the Big Brother house. Are you being sarcastic or was that a serious response? Curly thinks it may have been sarcastic.

You've got to look at the bigger picture, Essie and not worry too much about the small potatoes. Are you Australian? This wouldn't be a major stumbling block if you are.

Listen, I've got a whole load of wannabes who are queuing up to audition for me but what I'm really after is a bona fide trainer who doesn't really seek publicity. Incredibly your naive rejection to the career lifeline I handed you has actually enhanced your claims of being my unpaid personal trainer.

You'll have your own room and private space – I won't go in your room at all – unless invited. Who knows we might bond during the hours? My second divorce should be absolute very soon. If you have a boyfriend he could stay over occasionally. Maybe he could take a dislike to me and there could be a running theme of friction between us. I could slap a sex ban on the two of you.

Food wise you're the expert so you'll have full licence to choose and purchase what I'll be eating. I'm telling you now I don't like spinach and liver and under no circumstance would I want to eat those food matters.

Also I drink a lot of espresso coffee. Hopefully that won't be a problem.

Get back to me with your response. Have a think about things first.

Jot your stats down and a pic if you have one available.

Best regards,

Raymond Delauney

From:	"Essie Donovan" <essied@dsw.com>
To:	raymonddelauney@yahoo.co.uk
Subject:	RE: Cook and Trainer
Date:	Fri, 10 Feb 2006 10:19:01 -0800

Raymond,

No I am not nuts. And no I am not from Australia, try NY.

I am sure it is a good opportunity for you. How do I know that you are on the up and up as we say States side. I am a performer and have been for a very long time so I know a few things about the business. Plus I can not do anything that is non-union and unpaid, my own rule.

I've done things for no money in the past with a hope of "making it" needless to say I am a little wiser in my old age.

Now, since I am just back from a very bad back injury due to a fall in a show which kept me incapacitated for almost 6 months therefore I am not back in "camera" shape yet.

I am sure you will find someone to help you fulfill your reality dreams but I am afraid if there is no money to pay me I will be unable to help you better yourself.

Did you know that coffee is very bad for you? If I were going to help you that would be the first to go after the alcohol and the drugs...

Good luck again and thank you for thinking of me.

Essie D

Ps. Oh, I don't remember anywhere in my ad saying that I would clean up after anyone.

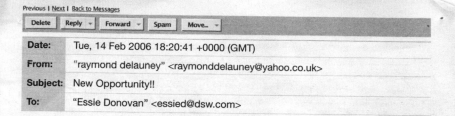

Date:	Tue, 14 Feb 2006 18:20:41 +0000 (GMT)
From:	"raymond delauney" <raymonddelauney@yahoo.co.uk>
Subject:	New Opportunity!!
To:	"Essie Donovan" <essied@dsw.com>

Hi Essie,

Thanks for getting back to me with your latest response.

To be perfectly candid I did find it a little puzzling. If you are not in "camera" shape does this mean you are carrying a few pounds extra? No real problems with that Essie, so am I! It's just that it would have looked a little silly being trained by someone who is as porky as me. Still, you must be a good cook!

Sorry to hear about your fall, I've taken a few tumbles in my time too – usually after a few drinks.

Raif's cooled on the idea of me being filmed whilst regaining my fitness. When we pitched the idea in his office on Friday I detected a discernible lack of interest on his part. After a few seconds pause all he did was light a More cigarette, put it to his lips before saying, "Too many fucking fitness shows about at the moment, Ray."

He might have mentioned this to me earlier before I'd been up all night editing the four-minute trailer. I also went to the expense of hiring an overhead projector.

In an odd sort of way I'm quite relieved, as I'm not sure I could do without coffee and cognac for a whole month.

It's not all doom and gloom though – Raif and myself went out to Grouchos later that night and we had a rare evening out. Several cognacs and cigars later we came up with the germ of a brilliant idea – and fingers crossed, our next film.

Date-a-Delauney.

I get together a list of 30 single women (ranging from the ages 21–45) as blind dates. I will not have met any of these girls beforehand. Each girl will hopefully be from a different country. All will be able to speak perfect English.

I will date a different girl every night at the same restaurant for a whole month. Each date will be secretly filmed and certain procedures will be consistent throughout.

I will pick each girl up in a limo, I will hand each date an expensive bouquet of flowers and at the end of the evening ask each girl back to my mansion for coffee and a swim. Various scenarios will be employed to add drama to the situation. For example on one occasion I'll attack another diner on an adjoining table after mistaking him for someone who slept with my ex-wife, another time some attractive women will hit on me in front of my date. Another scenario sees me stepping in and breaking up a fight between a big group of rugby louts, punching a few of them out. These set-ups are still being decided on and we'll be using paid actors on low rates.

I don't really have a mansion but for the purpose of the film I will be borrowing my friend's pad. He's gay and lives in a beautiful house in Belgravia, which has a Jacuzzi and a swimming pool. He is away in Monte Carlo for three months.

Myself and the crew will interview a series of real celebrities before the show, the likes of Richard Branson, Dennis Norden, Nigel Martyn and Paul Ross to make a series of predictions before the show. For example, how many women will slap me round the face? How many will refuse to pay for the meal? How many will sleep with me? How many dates walk out on me etc.

The whole show could serve as a case study on the way women around the world react in certain situations towards a regular guy like me. Each correct answer from our panel of celebs will see £100 go to a charity of their choice. This money will come from Channel 4 not me.

Would you fancy being my American date? If things worked out who knows what could become of it? I am single now and wouldn't necessarily be put off if you are a bit lumpy following your back problems. If you can see past a beer belly and a few extra chins you'll see before you a caring guy who takes his responsibilities seriously.

I'm pretty careful with money but not tight.

I can't promise anything definite without having first met you. As I'm sure you understand I'll also be meeting 29 other single women so it would be best to let you know my decision after the month's filming is complete. Raif is pretty much ready to sign the show off immediately and authorise us an advance on the budget.

The cost of the show will be relatively cheap as most of my productions are – the limo will be given to us free in exchange for publicity and the same thing shall apply as regards the flowers. We hope to use a top restaurant – but we are having problems finding a place that'll let us have free meals for two people for a whole month.

What I could do here is get the date to pay – I could pretend to have left my wallet at home. Otherwise this will cost our production company around 30 x £100, which works out as much as £3k.

I have a list of 14 provisional women from all round the world who have responded to my advert to date. Will you be okay to be my American date? Topics for conversation would be regular subjects like, Iraq, the Superbowl, obesity in the US, Simon Cowell etc. Incidentally, do you know of any South American women who want to be on telly? I've got a Brazilian.

I should add I have an 8-year-old son but he lives in Lowestoft with his mother and stepfather. I rarely get to see him as I work irregular hours, it's a long drive and the return journey costs around £50 in petrol. I've never missed a birthday and Raymond Junior is old enough to know who his real dad is – so that's the important thing.

Anyway, I've got a lot to organise so get back to me with a response as soon as possible and we'll take things from there.

Best regards,

Raymond

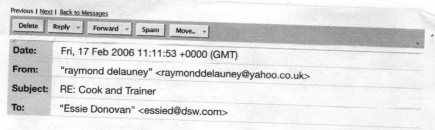

Delete	Reply ▾	Forward ▾	Spam	Move... ▾

Date:	Fri, 17 Feb 2006 11:11:53 +0000 (GMT)
From:	"raymond delauney" <raymonddelauney@yahoo.co.uk>
Subject:	RE: Cook and Trainer
To:	"Essie Donovan" <essied@dsw.com>

Essie,

I'm gonna have to push you for a reply or look elsewhere soon.

I'm holding off a redhead from Tallahassee.

Best regards,

Raymond

Delete   Reply ▾   Forward ▾   Spam   Move... ▾

From:	"Essie Donovan" <essied@dsw.com>
Sent:	17 February 2006 10:45:11
To:	raymonddelauney@yahoo.co.uk
Subject:	RE:

I am now back on the NY I do not think I will be returning to the UK.

Thank you for your persistence.

Essie

END OF CORRESPONDENCE

BIKE CHICKS

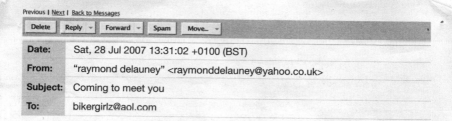

| Delete | Reply ▾ | Forward ▾ | Spam | Move... ▾ |

Date:	Sat, 28 Jul 2007 13:31:02 +0100 (BST)
From:	"raymond delauney" <raymonddelauney@yahoo.co.uk>
Subject:	Coming to meet you
To:	bikergirlz@aol.com

Hi,

Your website first came to my attention when I 'googled' the words women + bikers on my Apple MacBook Pro laptop (wireless).

I was bullied at school for reasons I won't go in to, so ideally I want to belong to a gang like yours to boost my reputation and feel protected without the threat of a man with a hairy back beating up on me.

I don't really go in for the traditional tattoo covered, liquor drinking, beating people up, Hell's Angel image because of my religious beliefs. I am also a vegetarian and underweight for my height. I simply want to ride a bike and belong to a gang. Yours is as good as any other, better probably. I'd have no problem with being in an all lesbian gang whatsoever.

I live in England and recently purchased my first ever bike, a baby blue 125 Yamaha 2 stroke and have two locks for it.

I have exceptionally skinny arms and as a result I lack muscular power. I like to go a steady 30–40 rather than risk violating any traffic regulations. My mom bought me the bike on the condition I do not speed. In Britain you can only travel at 30mph in built up areas.

I'd prefer to ride in your gang for the security of being in a group, it'll be my first time abroad. I know you have an all woman policy but I do have long hair. I could quite easily pass for a woman, especially when on a bike as I have skinny legs as well.

I get picked on quite a bit back at home so belonging to a butch gang of girls like yours who can handle themselves if necessary would give my mother some peace of mind. Obviously I wouldn't risk it with men's Hells Angels, as they'd probably beat me up.

I am also very keen on finding a girlfriend for my stay, maybe staying as penpals, no pressure but there must be someone in your gang who likes slim, longhaired English guys. I enjoy Tibetan poetry and table tennis.

Obviously I wouldn't make a pass at any of the leather dressed girls in the gang and would only speak when I'm spoken to. However I am single and if any of your girls are bisexual then I wouldn't rule anything out.

I'll arrive in September – could we arrange a meet with you and the gang?

All the best of British,

Raymond Delauney

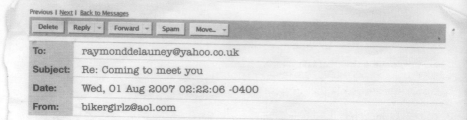

To: raymonddelauney@yahoo.co.uk

Subject: Re: Coming to meet you

Date: Wed, 01 Aug 2007 02:22:06 -0400

From: bikergirlz@aol.com

Regarding your personal issues & concerns, you would be better served by staying where you are & seeking professional counseling & psychiatric assistance.

You are completely misguided to think that any lesbian group will be of resource to you, as you are a man. You are not at all appropriate for inclusion in any lesbian group of any kind, much less a group of lesbian bikers.

Do not contact me again or any members of any lesbian bike groups again.

Thank you.

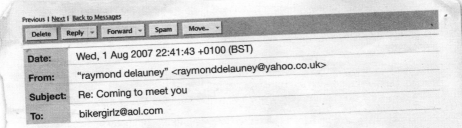

Date: Wed, 1 Aug 2007 22:41:43 +0100 (BST)

From: "raymond delauney" <raymonddelauney@yahoo.co.uk>

Subject: Re: Coming to meet you

To: bikergirlz@aol.com

Hi,

Thanks for taking the time to reply to me even if the message you sent was quite hostile in tone.

Actually, reading it back again I'm begining to get quite angry. I do belicvo I found it extremely offensive.

Where do you get off being so mean to someone who requests a meeting?

This is simply not how we do things here in England.

I do not discriminate against lesbians. In fact I try to be civil to people of either gender and bisexuals.

I might not be a dyke but I do have a bike.

Not all men are beasts you know contrary to what my aunt Gilda says.

I thought I could go for a ride with you when I visited America, that was all. When I'm on my bike I feel at ease with myself, completely free and alone, especially when part of a group.

Besides, some of the girls in the gang might want to get pregnant through artificial insemination (non sex) if we hit it off on a friendly basis and I could have been able to facilitate this.

As a personal favour to me please try and be less aggressive to the next person who has the misfortune to cross your path.

Disappointed,

Raymond Delauney

Delete   Reply ⌄   Forward ⌄   Spam   Move... ⌄

To:	raymonddelauney@yahoo.co.uk
Subject:	Re: Coming to meet you
Date:	Wed, 01 Aug 2007 19:51:20 -0400
From:	bikergirlz@aol.com

If this is NOT how you do things in England, (which I do know from my sisters in the UK, "IS" the way to respond to ignorant, self-serving English entitlement of a male chauvinist) then why in the world are you NOT inseminating & riding with any English lesbian biker clubs!!! You idiotic wimp... I would be shocked if anyone else of a lesbian group has given you anything but a tolerant "no thank you", or most likely in 90% of the cases of all who receive your ridiculous email, **NO REPLY** at all.

Raymond, I've hit you as hard as possible between the ears, (ideally to sink thru to your brain?), in written word to hopefully give you a WAKE UP call! Keep up this approach, & it's quite likely that some dyke, in an astonished, outraged reaction to your contemptible assumptions, will not only humiliate you, she'll quite possibly be compelled to provide you with the beating you're obviously really seeking, only, (or so you say) not at the hands of a man... hmm...

How typical of "male privilege" mentality that as you attempt to play the victim of your circumstances, then feel obliged to keep the hostility going, which YOU warranted with your non-consensual, unsolicited, UNACCEPTABLE email reply! You infringed upon my/our dyke's club's privacy & then feel you need to email me AGAIN to further argue why you think any dyke biker should somehow respond to save you from yourself(!)... to be polite to you(!), to allow YOU more comfort in YOUR male world!

Obviously you've done little to nothing to understand what you could do to make things better for how men "USE" women, but instead default to the "poor little me" mindset. You're demonstrating typical male mentality in minimizing how your ignorant assumptions affect women, as you feel so inclined to infringe on "FEMALE ENERGY ONLY" space.

IF you are indeed a transgendered female identity as a male bodied person who does not yet have enough self esteem to pursue your own rightful place in the world, then that it is an entirely different conversation. In this case, once again I strongly suggest that your traveling money would be much better spent seeking psychiatric support. Thus far, you've done nothing more than to demonstrate how deeply in need you are of at least "social conscious" counseling...

NEWS FLASH!!!: You are NOT allowed to do so at the expense of other, braver than you are, female human beings who have the courage to live life in less than an ideal world, (where WE TOO have had to face the physical brutality of men BY OURSELVES, unless we honorably banded together to appropriately seek to HELP OTHER WOMEN) who you obviously think you're entitled to harass because I failed to modal cuddle you in your "oh whoa is me" mentality.

Speaking of "personal favors"! Favors are granted to someone who's not an offense to the one being asked the favor of.

So address accurate perspective on the concept of "personal favor", DO YOURSELF ONE! *STOP* your actions, thoughts & behavior that allows you to some how stay in HUGE DENIAL that you're somehow entitled to the right to violate women/dyke/lesbian/female body identity only space & ACCESS! I'd put money on the fact that no lesbian worth her salt will be asking YOU for sperm donor contributions.

Pleeeease wake up & do some realistic self-care, for your well being, & to assist your mother with her concerns for you, get HELP from a psychiatric professional.

I'm not concerned about further contact from you, as I've now blocked you from any further contact.

Signed,

"Revolted", by your Male Chavenism "Insanity"

END OF CORRESPONDENCE

LITERARY AGENT

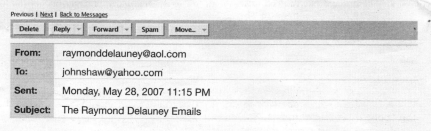

Delete | **Reply** ▼ | **Forward** ▼ | **Spam** | **Move...** ▼

From: raymonddelauney@aol.com

To: johnshaw@yahoo.com

Sent: Monday, May 28, 2007 11:15 PM

Subject: The Raymond Delauney Emails

Hi John,

I've been told yours is one of the best literary agencies in the business.

Okay, so I made that first line up just to grab your attention.

Anyway, so I'm sending you my hysterically funny masterpiece of a manuscript in the hope you can tell me (straight) whether it is something you think has the potential to go to print.

I'm hoping you won't be as rude as some of the other guys. I sent the manuscript off to one firm with the disclaimer "This book does not bear any resemblance to any person living or dead" and they sent it back with the note, "yeah, that's what's wrong with it".

Very briefly, The Raymond Delauney Emails is a collection of genuine e-mails sent to a variety of people along with their equally authentic responses. Inspired by the wonderful Henry Root letters (aka William Donaldson), the wet fish merchant from Elm Park Mansions, SW10.

Raymond Delauney is a harder nosed, less tolerant, infinitely more irritating individual. He poses variously as a job applicant, a salesman, an inventor, an entrepreneur, and always, a royal pain in the arse.

Synopsis and manuscript are attached.

Hope to hear from you soon,

Raymond

From:	johnshaw@yahoo.com
To:	raymonddelauney@aol.com
Sent:	Tuesday, May 29, 2007 09:35 AM
Subject:	The Raymond Delauney Emails

Dear Mr Delauney,

I don't open attachments from strangers or read online; email is for inquiries. I'm afraid that, in any event, my list is closed and I don't handle novelties or practical joke material of the kind you seem to be proposing. I confess, also, that the slightly complaining or injured tone behind the surface of your email would discourage me even if you were proposing a different kind of book.

Apologies, JS

From:	raymonddelauney@aol.com
To:	johnshaw@yahoo.com
Sent:	Thu, May 31, 2007 13:15 PM
Subject:	The Raymond Delauney Emails

Hiya John,

Thanks for your mail, the most unambiguous 'no' I'm likely to receive. I hope.

I do appreciate you getting back to me (most polite) and fully understand your policy of not opening attachments online. And also the fact you don't handle the sort of material I was proposing.

I'm sorry if you thought my mail adopted either a 'slightly complaining' or indeed an 'injured' tone. But that's the thing with tones, in emails at least – they can be misinterpreted. My pitch was intended to be light and funny, like the manuscript itself.

All the best,

Ray

P.S. The line below in the original mail was a joke and not actually a genuine complaint!

I'm hoping you won't be as rude as some of the other guys. I sent the manuscript off to one firm with the disclaimer "This book does not bear any resemblance to any person living or dead" and they sent it back with the note, "yeah, that's what's wrong with it".

| Delete | Reply ▾ | Forward ▾ | Spam | Move... ▾ |

From:	johnshaw@yahoo.com
To:	raymonddelauney@aol.com
Sent:	Thursday, May 31, 2007 14:07 PM
Subject:	The Raymond Delauney Emails

I know that you didn't intend a wrong tone. That's why I warned you. Good luck, JS

END OF CORRESPONDENCE

TOMBSTONE

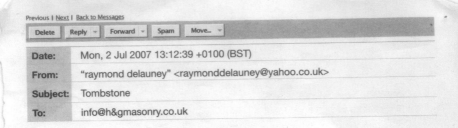

Delete   Reply ▾   Forward ▾   Spam   Move... ▾

Date:	Mon, 2 Jul 2007 13:12:39 +0100 (BST)
From:	"raymond delauney" <raymonddelauney@yahoo.co.uk>
Subject:	Tombstone
To:	info@h&gmasonry.co.uk

Hi,

I understand you're in the business of making gravestones.

I need one to use for when I am dead.

You guys must earn good money judging by the estimates I'm getting back which are nearly enough to make me keel over.

I know someone who works as a gravedigger but he says he can't get me discount. He tells everyone down the pub he has 'a lot of people working under him'. That gag wears a bit thin after you hear it four times every week.

I'm at the age where I've got more years behind me than in front. So I've been working on a funny epitaph for my headstone. Basically I want to stick two fingers up at the world, more specifically at my estranged family.

Do you do any other headstone colours to grey? I'd really like something garish. Do cemeteries have any rules on this? I suppose they must.

I've fallen out with my family. I've been divorced twice and the kids I stayed in touch with from the second marriage sided against me and with their mother when I fell in love with a younger woman. The kids don't come and see me anymore so I have disowned them. The new wife has also gone back to Thailand now so it was all for nothing.

One thing is for certain. The kids will attend the reading of the will.

And that will come as a grave disappointment to them.

More so than I ever was.

Everyone thinks I'm minted since I live in a big house and worked as a stockbroker. I did retire with a juicy pay off but the house is rented, my windfall has been banana frittered away, gambling is my big weakness.

I've squandered all my money on gambling, women and marvel comics. I have one of the largest collections of superhero comics in the country – all in pristine condition. It is worth several thousand pounds but I will NEVER sell them. I shall either leave them to a fellow collector or a cats' home just to aggravate the dependants at the reading of the will. I plan on having it videoed, not by me, obviously.

Could you kindly give me a quote on the cost of the headstone with the attached four-line inscription.

Please use your cheapest stone and provide me a range of sizes.

Thanks

R. Delauney

| Delete | Reply ▾ | Forward ▾ | Spam | Move... ▾ |

From:	"H&G" <info@ h&gmasonry.co.uk>
To:	"raymond delauney" <raymonddelauney@yahoo.co.uk>
Subject:	Re: Tombstone
Date:	Mon, 2 Jul 2007 13:51:29 +0100

Please find attached a rough mock up shown on 16" x 8" marble which would be £82 delivered (UK mainland)

Kind Regards
Barry Pringle
H&G Masonry

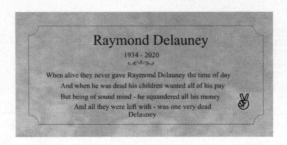

END OF CORRESPONDENCE